How to Become a
Forensic Psychologist

Jo Bailey, Julie Harrower†
and Dee Anand

R Routledge
Taylor & Francis Group

LONDON AND NEW YORK

Designed cover image: Getty Images

First published 2026
by Routledge
4 Park Square, Milton Park, Abingdon, Oxon OX14 4RN

and by Routledge
605 Third Avenue, New York, NY 10158

Routledge is an imprint of the Taylor & Francis Group, an informa business

© 2026 Jo Bailey, Julie Harrower and Dee Anand

The right of Jo Bailey, Julie Harrower and Dee Anand to be identified as authors of this work has been asserted in accordance with sections 77 and 78 of the Copyright, Designs and Patents Act 1988.

British Library Cataloguing-in-Publication Data
A catalogue record for this book is available from the British Library

ISBN: 978-1-138-93814-4 (hbk)
ISBN: 978-1-138-93815-1 (pbk)
ISBN: 978-1-315-67583-1 (ebk)

DOI: 10.4324/9781315675831

Typeset in Galliard
by Apex CoVantage, LLC

Access the Instructor and Student Resources: www.routledgetextbooks.com/textbooks/howtopsy/

How to Become a Forensic Psychologist

Forensic psychology has grown significantly in recent years, with increasing numbers of professionals working in the field. This practical and accessible resource contains all the information and advice required by those considering pursuing a career in the sector.

How do you qualify as a forensic psychologist, and what is the job really like? This is the first guide to a role we usually only see through the lens of television or film dramas. It provides an overview of what the job involves, the educational qualifications and training you will need, and what those first few years in the job are actually like. Including tips on how to make the most of opportunities available, the book also features testimonials from forensic psychologists, plus information on related career paths.

How to Become a Forensic Psychologist is authored by leading forensic psychologists in the United Kingdom. It is the perfect companion for anyone considering this exciting career, from A-level students and undergraduates with an interest in the discipline to anyone considering a career change.

This book is one of seven in the *How to Become a Practitioner Psychologist* series, each covering a different psychology career. The other titles in the series can be found here: www.routledgetextbooks.com/textbooks/howtopsy/

Jo Bailey, OBE, is the chief psychologist in His Majesty's Prison and Probation Service (HMPPS) covering England and Wales.

Julie Harrower† was Associate Dean in the Faculty of Health and Life Sciences at Coventry University, UK.

Dee Anand is a consultant Forensic Psychologist and former Chair of the National Division of Forensic Psychology; former head of Qualification in Forensic Psychology in the UK; a specialist member of the Parole Board in England and Wales and a Parole Commissioner in Northern Ireland.

How to Become a Practitioner Psychologist

Series Editor: David Murphy

Psychology remains one of the most popular choices for an under-graduate degree, whilst an increasing number of postgraduate courses are directed either towards further academic study in a sub-discipline, or a career in applied practice. But despite the growing numbers of people interested in a career in psychology, from A-level students to those looking for a career change, the various pathways to entry into the profession are not necessarily obvious.

The *How to Become a Practitioner Psychologist* series of books is aimed at providing a clear, accessible and reader-friendly guide to the routes available to becoming a practitioner psychologist. Providing both information and advice, including testimonials from those recently qualified, the series will include a title for each of the 7 domains of psychology practice as regulated by the Health and Care Professions Council.

Each book in the series will provide an invaluable introduction to anyone considering a career in this fascinating profession.

David Murphy FBPsS, FRSA is Emeritus Professor of Clinical Psychology at the University of Plymouth, UK. He has been programme director of the clinical psychology programmes at the University of Oxford, UK, and University of Plymouth, UK. He served as the 2019–20 President of the British Psychological Society (BPS) having previously served as Chair of the BPS Professional Practice Board and been Director of the Professional Standards Unit of the BPS Division of Clinical Psychology.

How to Become a Forensic Psychologist
Jo Bailey, Julie Harrower and Dee Anand

How to Become a Clinical Psychologist
Laura Golding and Judith Moss

www.routledgetextbooks.com/textbooks/howtopsy/

'In memory of Julie Harrower'

Contents

Introduction

David Murphy – Series Editor

Welcome!

I would like to welcome you to this book, which is one of a series of seven titles, each of which focuses on a different type of practitioner psychologist registered as a professional in the United Kingdom. One of the things that have always appealed to me about psychology is its incredible diversity; even within my own field of clinical psychology, there is a vast range of client groups and ways of working. The books in this series are all written by practitioner psychologists who are not only experts in, but also hugely enthusiastic about, their areas of practice. This series presents a fascinating insight into the nature of each domain, the range of activities and the approaches within it, and also the fantastic variety there is across the different areas of practice. However, we have also made sure that we have answered the practical questions you may have, such as '*How long does it take to train?*', '*What do I need to do to get on a training course?*' and '*How secure will my income be at the end of it all?*'. We very much hope that this book will be interesting and answer all your questions (even ones you didn't know you had!), and further information and resources are available on our series website (www.routledge.com/cw/howtobecomeapractitionerpsychologist).

Psychology as a Profession

Psychology is still a relatively young profession compared to many long-established professions such as law, medicine and accounting; however, it has grown incredibly rapidly over the last few decades. One of the

DOI: 10.4324/9781315675831-1

first people to use the title 'Psychologist' in a professional context was an American named Lightner Witmer, who, just over a hundred years ago, established what is widely recognised as the world's first psychology clinic in Pennsylvania. Witmer came to study psychology after completing a first degree in economics and postgraduate studies in political science, and then working for a time as a schoolteacher. He went on to study experimental psychology at the University of Pennsylvania and then at a famous research laboratory in Leipzig, Germany. He subsequently became a pioneer applying experimental psychology ideas to the treatment of children with specific learning and speech difficulties.

At the beginning of the twentieth century, these early psychologists saw great possibilities in applying psychological concepts to help people achieve their potential. However, even they could scarcely imagine the scale and range of applications of psychology that would exist by the beginning of the twenty-first century. Psychologists now have well-established roles in schools, mental and physical health services, prisons, police and security services, multinational companies and sports training centres, essentially almost anywhere where there is a focus on understanding and changing human behaviour, which, of course, is pretty much everywhere!

This book, along with the other six titles in the series, is intended to provide people who are at the beginning of their careers, or those who are thinking about making a change, an insight into the different areas of professional psychology. We hope that you will gain not only an overview of the specific domain of psychology it entails but also a sense of what it is like to work as a practitioner on a day-to-day basis. We also aim to explain how to become qualified to practise in the area of professional psychology, all the way from school until being fully qualified. Furthermore, we hope to provide an idea of how careers in the different areas of psychology can develop over time and how the profession of psychology might change as it continues to develop in the future.

Studying Psychology at School or College

One thing that many people (me included) love about psychology is just how broad it is. As an academic discipline, it encompasses the physiological workings of the brain and the nervous system, how we perceive sounds and language, how we make decisions and the treatment of mental health problems, to name just a few areas. In recent years, psychology has become the second most popular first-degree subject at UK universities; indeed, figures from the Higher Education Statistical Agency (HESA) show that a total of 90,000 students were studying, either full-time or part-time, for an undergraduate degree in psychology in the academic year 2022–2023.

Psychology has also become not only a popular A-level choice but also increasingly an option at the General Certificate of Secondary Education (GCSE) level. It is, therefore, now possible to take the first step on a career journey in psychology at an early age, and, if you are considering A-level or GCSE subjects, we would certainly encourage you to look at psychology options if they are offered at your school. However, it is by no means required to have studied psychology at either GCSE or A-level in order to follow a career in psychology. If psychology isn't offered at your school, or you opt to go for other subjects, this won't stop you from going on to become a psychologist, if you decide that this is what you would like to do. On the other hand, contrary to some myths, psychology is considered a valid A-level choice for many other degrees apart from psychology; indeed, it is listed as a 'preferred subject' by University College London in their general list of A-level subject choices www.ucl.ac.uk/prospective-students/undergraduate/application/requirements/preferred-a-level-subjects.

The only GCSE subjects that are specifically required by UK universities for studying psychology are maths and English. A-level Psychology is usually listed as a 'preferred' subject but is currently not required by any UK university for entry to a psychology degree course, and there is no indication that this will change. Therefore, our advice would be that psychology is an interesting subject choice, which can provide a good foundation for further study in psychology or other subjects. However, psychology at A-level is by no means essential for a career as a psychologist, so we recommend basing the decision on what your strengths and interests are and also what subjects are required for any other degree options you want to keep open to you.

Routes Into Graduate Psychology Careers

The first compulsory step on the road to a psychology career is attaining 'Graduate Basis for Chartered Membership' of the BPS, commonly known as 'GBC' (in the past, this was called 'Graduate Basis for Registration' or 'GBR' for short). You will see this referred to a number of times in this book and the other titles in the series. The BPS is the professional body and learnt society for psychology in the United Kingdom. It was established in 1901 to promote both academic and applied psychology and currently has over 60,000 members, making it one of the largest psychological societies in the world. There are two possible routes to attain the GBC of the BPS based on the UK qualifications.

A Psychology Undergraduate Degree

The most common route is to complete an undergraduate degree in psychology that is accredited by the BPS; a lower second-class degree classification or above is required for GBC. This doesn't need to be a single honours degree in psychology; it can be a joint degree with another subject. However, in order to be accredited, it has to cover a core curriculum that is specified by the BPS, and the provision must meet certain other standards. At the time of writing, there are 839 BPS-accredited undergraduate courses offered at 126 different universities within the United Kingdom. Many of these courses are general psychology degrees; however, some focus more on specific domains such as forensic psychology, health psychology, abnormal psychology, sports psychology and business psychology. About a third of all accredited undergraduate programmes are offered as a psychology combined with another subject, and the array of possible options is extensive, including business, English literature, education, maths, history, philosophy, physics, zoology and criminology. This range of choice could be a bit overwhelming, but it is important to bear in mind that virtually all psychology degrees do offer a significant choice of options within them, so two students doing the same generic psychology degree at the same institution may actually take quite a different mix of courses, albeit still with the same core psychology components. Moreover, it is also important to remember that even if the title of a degree appears very specific, the course will still cover the same core psychology content if it is BPS accredited.

For a career in professional psychology, the most important issue is attaining GBC; the subtle differences in the individual course content are far less important. Our advice would be to consider all the factors that are important to you about the choice of university and the psychology course rather than getting too focused on the specific content of a course. You may wish to do a degree that allows you to specialise in the area of psychology that you are particularly interested in, and of course, that's fine. However, in reality, all postgraduate professional training courses need to cater to people with a range of different psychology backgrounds, so whilst having done specialised options at the undergraduate level might provide a good foundation to build on, it's very unlikely to mean you can jump ahead of those who didn't do those options at the undergraduate level.

My own experience was that I did a joint degree with psychology and zoology (I have to confess that I wasn't really sure what psychology was when I was choosing, so I hedged my bets!). Fairly early on, I became interested in clinical psychology, but I still got a great deal out of studying other subjects that weren't anything to do with clinical psychology, including many of the zoology subjects. In my final year, I did an option in vertebrate palaeontology (better known as the study of dinosaurs!) mainly because it sounded interesting. In fact, it turned out to be one of the most stimulating and useful courses I have ever studied, and the lecturer was one of the best teachers I ever had. I learnt how to interpret inconclusive evidence by using careful observation and deduction, rather than jumping to conclusions, and that generic skill has been very useful throughout my clinical psychology career. So, my personal advice would be not to feel under any pressure to specialise in a particular branch of psychology too soon. I suggest you choose degree options because they are stimulating and well taught, *not* because you think they will look good on your CV. In reality, if you are applying for professional psychology training courses, what will stand out more on your CV will be really good grades, which in turn come from being highly engaged and developing a thorough understanding of the areas you are studying.

Some psychology programmes offer a 'professional placement year' within the degree. Such courses are often marketed on the basis that graduates have a higher employment rate on graduation; however, it is important to bear in mind that you will also be graduating a year later than people on a three-year course, and during the placement year, most people will be receiving little or no pay and still paying fees (albeit at a reduced rate) to the university. My own personal opinion is that degrees with professional placements don't necessarily offer a significant advantage overall. On the one hand, if the course does have well-established placement opportunities, this can make it easier to get that first step on the ladder; however, there are many opportunities for getting postgraduate experience relevant to professional psychology, some of which are voluntary but many of which are paid.

Choosing a University to Study Psychology

As well as choosing a specific course, you will also need to choose individual universities to apply to. A detailed consideration of the different universities offering undergraduate psychology programmes is beyond the scope of this series, and there is also a great deal of information freely available on the web (starting with the University College Admissions Service (UCAS) website) and from schools and colleges. However, it is true to say that universities do vary somewhat, and, of course, the local area in which they are located is also a factor to consider. The Unistats website (www.unistats.com) is the official website providing data gathered from the National Student Survey and other independent sources, which can be used for comparing universities and individual courses. One particular issue that prospective applicants can be confused about is what is meant by a university being in the 'Russell Group' and what the significance of this is. The Russell Group is a self-selected association of 24 research-intensive universities across the United Kingdom that was formed in 1994. Although they only account for 15% of all UK higher education institutions, Russell Group universities receive nearly 80% of all UK research funding. However, it does not necessarily follow that it is always better to do your psychology degree at a Russell Group university; indeed, some of the most highly rated universities for psychology, such as the University of Bath and the University of St Andrews, were not members of the Russell Group at the time of writing. Whilst it is understandable to think that going for a well-known name or the Russell Group 'brand name' must be a safe bet, in order to find the best fit for YOU, there really is no alternative to doing a bit of research into individual universities and the specific course options they offer and then going to visit to get the feel of the institution and the local area. After all, you will be investing three (or in some cases, four) years of your life in this decision, so although it's certainly not something to stress out excessively about, it is worth putting a bit of time into.

University Applications

Once you have chosen universities and specific courses you wish to apply for, you will need to apply via the UCAS website (www.ucas.com). The site contains a great deal of advice, and you should also access the advice available from your school or college. One of the things you will be required to do is to submit a personal statement (PS). The UCAS website has comprehensive general information on writing a PS, including a mind map and worksheet. The key principles of writing a PS are the same regardless of what course you are applying for, that is, demonstrating you understand what the subject is about, conveying why you are interested in it, and demonstrating that you have the skills required to successfully complete the course and make a positive contribution to the learning process. Providing evidence of things you have done, which demonstrate your interest, enthusiasm and abilities, will inevitably carry more weight than simply saying, 'I am passionate about psychology'. Furthermore, admission tutors will also pay attention to how well-structured and well-written your PS itself is since academic writing ability is important to success as a psychology undergraduate. If at this stage you are particularly interested in one career path within professional psychology, then you will certainly want to mention this, although it would also be helpful to demonstrate that you understand what the career path involves and that an undergraduate degree is one step towards this. Sometimes, people's own experience of mental health or emotional difficulties or that of a close friend or family member has influenced their interest in psychology and/or pursuing a career in psychology. Again, don't feel shy about mentioning this, although only if you feel comfortable doing so. However, don't lose sight of the purpose of the PS and what an admission tutor will be looking for; lived experience can really help to understand the perspective of people with psychological difficulties, but you will need to cover the other skills required. Furthermore, since psychology is such a broad subject, it's important to bear in mind that you will need to study a whole range of topics, most of which will be unrelated to any one specific psychological problem. The UCAS website has a useful article about writing a PS for a psychology degree application (www. ucas.com/applying/applying-university/personal-statement-guides/ personal-statement-advice-psychology). If you are studying for, or have completed, a psychology degree at a university outside of the United Kingdom, then your course will not have been accredited by the BPS (at the time of writing, the BPS does accredit a small number of under-graduate programmes delivered outside the United Kingdom, but these have to be awarded by a UK university). However, it is possible to apply for GBC on the basis of a psychology degree undertaken any-where in the world, and the applications are assessed on an individual basis to establish whether the criteria are met (for further information, see www.bps.org.uk/membership/graduate-membership).

Converting to Psychology With a Degree in a Different Subject

People who have completed a first degree other than psychology (or those whose psychology degree did not meet the criteria for GBC) can still pursue a career in professional psychology; this route involves attaining GBC by doing a conversion course. At the time of writing, there were 126 BPS-accredited conversion courses at 88 different universities in the United Kingdom. Most of these lead to an MSc, although some lead to a graduate diploma; most are quite general in their content and are titled simply 'psychology' or 'applied psychology', whereas others are more focused on specific areas like child develop-ment, mental health, or even fashion. However, if they are BPS accred-ited, all of these conversion courses will still cover the core psychology curriculum regardless of their title.

Since the core components are common between all BPS-accredited degree programmes, you certainly will not be committing yourself irre-vocably to any one area of professional psychology through your choice of psychology undergraduate or postgraduate conversion course. In the clinical psychology programmes which I have run, we have taken people with a range of different experiences at the undergraduate level and many who completed different first degrees altogether. Of course, when you come to postgraduate qualifications, you do have to make more fundamental choices about the area of psychology you wish to focus on.

The Different Areas of Psychology Practice

The authors of each of the seven books in the series are, as you would expect, experts in, and very enthusiastic about, their own area of psychology practice, and the rest of this book will focus pretty much exclusively on this specific area. Our aim across the series is to provide information about what each domain is about, what it is like to work in this area on a day-to-day basis and what the route to become qualified is like. What we have not done, and indeed could not do, is say which one of the domains is 'best'. The answer is that there is no one 'best' type of psychologist; instead, we hope you will be able to find which area of practice seems to fit your own interests and strengths best. This can be difficult, and we would encourage you to keep an open mind for as long as you can; you might be surprised to find that an area you hadn't really thought much about seems to be a good fit.

Once you have identified an area of practice that seems to fit you best, we would certainly recommend that you try and meet people who work in that area and talk to them personally. Even after you have embarked on postgraduate training in a particular field, don't feel it's too late to explore other areas. Indeed, there are areas of overlap between the different domains so that psychologists with different training backgrounds might well end up working in a similar area. For instance, clinical and counselling psychologists often work together in psychological therapy services in the National Health Service (NHS), whereas health psychologists and occupational psychologists might work alongside each other in implementing employee health programmes.

My own journey in professional psychology started with my degree in psychology and zoology postgraduate training in clinical psychology, and then working in the NHS. However, my journey also included becoming registered as a health psychologist and a clinical neuropsychologist, and I went on to do management training and becoming a senior manager in the NHS before moving into clinical psychology training and then research in leadership development. Over the years,

I have worked alongside colleagues from all of the domains at various times, particularly through my roles with the BPS. I have been fascinated to learn even more about other domains through editing this series, and, of course, as psychology is still such a young and dynamic field, new developments continue to emerge – you may become a Lightner Witmer for the twenty-first century – pioneering a new application of psychology that no one has even thought of yet! I would therefore encourage you to think carefully about your career direction. However, whether your psychology 'career' lasts just for the duration of this book or for the rest of your working life, I would encourage you to maintain an open curious mind; in the words of one of my favourite sayings, '*It is better to travel well than to arrive*'. We hope this book and others in this series will be of help to you wherever your own unique career journey takes you.

2 | What Does a Forensic Psychologist Do?

- Profile of the role – what does a forensic psychologist do?
- What types of people do they work with?
- What types of environment do they work in?
- What qualities are required?
- What is the career trajectory?

Forensic Psychology

Forensic psychology deals with the psychological aspects of legal processes; this can include applying theory to criminal investigations, understanding psychological theory associated with criminal behaviour, and the treatment of offenders or those at risk of offending. You might hear people speak about a 'criminal psychologist', a 'legal psychologist', a 'criminologist' or a 'profiler'. Not all of these terms refer to psychologists or to those with psychological training. The psychologist title that covers all these areas is *forensic psychologist*, which is a 'protected title' in the United Kingdom.

In short, forensic psychology is applying psychology to criminal justice settings (CJS), and we'll outline more about this over the coming chapters.

Interest in Forensic Psychology

It is not uncommon to hear that people who were initially attracted to the profession of forensic psychology are attracted for all the wrong reasons! We have heard some say that they wanted to learn about 'criminal

DOI: 10.4324/9781315675831-2

behaviour' so they could eventually commit the 'perfect crime'. We have also heard people say they want to go inside the 'mind of a psychopath', and of course, there are those who have watched far too many television programmes or films, which portray forensic psychologists in a certain way. It is true that it may appear to be a unique and somewhat mysterious profession at first glance. But it is also true that TV programmes like 'Cracker' (in the old days), CSI or 'Law and Order' have forensic psychology themes or daring forensic psychologist protagonists. In reality, it is a rarity that forensic psychologists are heroic, death-defying, brave mavericks who solve crimes within convenient 60 minutes allowing for ad breaks. However, it is true that it is a rewarding, fascinating and challenging profession, where you meet people you might not otherwise meet in everyday life, you engage with theories understanding and explaining complex and challenging behaviour and you help to understand why people might do what they do, what the chances are that they might do something similar in the future and try to help them change or make different choices, or help the wider world understand the complex reasons behind decisions people might make.

On the one hand, the coverage in entertainment and the media has raised awareness of forensic psychology, but what people see on the television and the reality of working life does not always match. Television portrayal tends to focus on police work, with the forensic psychologists assisting at crime scenes, 'profiling' potential perpetrators and often even assisting in the arrest. In reality, our working life tends not to be quite so dramatic, although such work is available. There is much more to the role of a forensic psychologist, and deciding on the type of work you want to be involved in is one of the many choices you will need to make along the way. Whichever route you end up choosing, you are sure to experience a uniquely challenging profession – and you will need to develop your resilience, as that, together with your understanding of, and attitude to, social justice and change, will underpin everything you do. You are going to hear stories of people who have done some very bad things but who themselves may be very complex, often experienced trauma but have caused harm to others too. It is sometimes difficult to hear but rewarding when you know you are doing your best to help society. If you are interested in why people might make decisions which have resulted in challenging situations for themselves or others and indeed, how society has contributed to those decisions, then this might well be the profession for you. This is particularly true if you find that you want to help those people and, in turn, help society and help the community in which you live.

To understand the value of this profession, it is important to understand the magnitude of the situation we face. Crime has a significant impact on society and the quality of life for those within it. Police-recorded figures for violent crime have been increasing, as have those for sexual offences. Many people are direct victims of crime, or have friends or family who have been victimised. Working with people who have committed crimes, those who present with difficult or challenging behaviour and those who are in prison and/or at risk of further antisocial or criminal behaviour is the 'bread and butter' of a forensic psychologist's work. But this work is complex. We have a number of 'clients'; for example, it may be the offender, the victim, the police or all three. Everything we do must be defensible and based on evidence so we can justify our own decisions, which often come under significant scrutiny, whether we are working with offenders who have committed serious crimes or those whose offences are perceived as less serious.

Criminal justice policy and process can vary, resulting in changes to sentencing or bringing new offences into legislation or decriminalising other actions. The context within which forensic psychologists work is therefore often altering, influenced by policymakers, the government and other criminal justice agencies' actions.

Whilst sentences for violent and/or sexual offences vary widely depending on a range of circumstances and can include community service and/or probation, the prison population in England and Wales was 82, 676 in July 2019, with around 5% of the population women. This reduced to 79,092 in December 2021 with the decrease thought to be partially due to the COVID pandemic and the reduction in court activity with a similar proportion of women. The UK prison population is routinely around 95% male, so we see a striking difference between the numbers of men and women in prison. Thailand has the highest percentage of female prisoners (12% at the time of writing), but globally, the proportion of women amongst prisoners is typically below 7%. This is relevant not only in the type of work forensic psychologists might engage in but also in relation to the forensic psychologists themselves. As we will see later, currently many more women are employed as forensic psychologists than men. This is in part due to the greater number of women taking psychology courses in general in the United Kingdom, but it raises issues when working with a predominantly male population.

Incidentally, as of June 2024, in England and Wales, the total number in custody is currently around 87, 000, with around 24,000 more under the Probation Service in the community. The prison population has almost doubled over the past 25 years.

Perhaps it is worth starting with some definitions.

Firstly, there are some myths to dispel:

- Forensic psychology is <u>not</u> forensic science. If you are interested in the 'hard' science that goes with crime scene evidence, then forensic science is the route for you
- Profiling (also known as behavioural investigative advice or BIA) with the police is not the core work of a forensic psychologist. Whilst it does occur, it is less standard and only a small proportion of forensic psychologists are involved in this type of work. It makes for good TV and a very useful element to a film script but in real life, it is not in the normal day-to-day business of your average non-heroic forensic psychologist.
- Forensic psychiatry and forensic psychology are very different things. Forensic psychiatry requires medical training and is a specialised branch of psychiatry working mainly with mentally disordered offenders.

The BPS website describes psychology as:

> *the scientific study of the mind and how it dictates and influences our behaviour, from communication and memory to thought and emotion. It's about understanding what makes people tick and how this understanding can help us address many of the problems and issues in society today*.[1]

The Division of Forensic Psychology defines forensic psychology as:

> *the application of psychology within the legal system to create safer communities and to assist people to find pathways away from criminal behaviour. . . . In practice this means Forensic Psychologists assess,*

formulate and intervene in those engaging in harmful behaviours, provide advice and expertise to other professionals, and develop and facilitate training and knowledge in forensic settings all with the ultimate goal of contributing to the development of a safer society'.[2]

But frankly, that is a rather boring definition for what can be a very exciting and rewarding job and one which differs from other fields of psychology by exploring an interaction across different types of 'risk'. It doesn't all happen in prisons either. Almost everyone we work with presents some type of 'risk', and it is our job to understand that risk, help manage it and seek to reduce it whenever we can so that the person we are working with (as well as broader society) can benefit. To do this, we need to really get to grips with the psychology of behaviour and understand what has contributed to a person acting in the way they do. This goes beyond diagnosis and beyond thinking about people by asking the question 'what's wrong with them' and moves us to a place where we are better off asking, 'what has happened to them' and 'how has their interpretation of things led to them acting in the way they have done'. That is us thinking like psychologists.

In practice, forensic psychology is concerned with:

* *The application of psychological theory to criminal behaviour*
* *The exploration of what makes people commit crimes*
* *The application of psychology specialities to the legal/criminal justice arena*
* *The intersection between <u>psychology</u> and the <u>justice system</u>.*

So, what is the forensic psychology approach to the concept of risk? Forensic psychologists use a 'tripartite' approach to understanding the risk of a particular behaviour occurring – namely the risk of recidivism (reoffending), the risk of harm to self or others and the risk of mental deterioration.

Where forensic psychology is at its strongest and most unique is in considering the relationship between all of these approaches to predicting and understanding behaviour and decision-making. We take a 'clinical' approach to understanding motivations, behaviours and decisions and try to account for a variety of factors in understanding someone's actions. This includes understanding more about their background, childhood, personality and mental health, significant events which might have happened in their lives, environment and context – and the impact of these elements on their decisions and actions. This enables forensic psychologists to formulate an understanding which helps us to come up with approaches to intervention, treatment or ways to help people not repeat difficult or challenging behaviours. This approach also helps us to develop ideas, models and theories of understanding to prevent harmful behaviours from occurring in the first place. This way of understanding also enables forensic psychologists to help people stop from repeating these harmful behaviours or perhaps reduce their frequency or severity, and more often than not we will work with other professions to help achieve this. The forensic psychologist's role in formulating this understanding of a person and their behaviours is a crucial aspect in helping to manage the risk someone might pose, but this is always best managed in combination with other professionals. After all, many heads are often better than one, but we are able to show leadership from an evidence-based approach. All of this basically means we try to use our knowledge, theory and experience to work out why people do bad things and how we can help to stop it from happening again!

So, as we started this chapter, broadly, whilst there will be subtle changes to the definition of the role of a forensic psychologist dependent on whichever definition best suits the eventual role and environment one works in, forensic psychology is psychology applied within some form of legal or CJS, for a range of purposes which this book will touch on. We do not go into depth about psychological theory here but will reference a range of useful introductory texts and publications.

The Health and Care Professions Council (HCPC) is the regulating body for all practitioner psychologists, including forensic psychologists, and in order to practise independently, individuals must register with the HCPC. To do this, we need to meet the standards set by the HCPC for the profession in order to demonstrate 'fitness to practice'. To register, you must successfully complete an approved programme of study, which will show that you meet the HCPC professional standards and are thus eligible to apply for registration. Prior to the involvement of the HCPC, the BPS was the only regulatory body for qualified forensic psychologists. When we talk about forensic psychologists here, we mean those registered and no longer under training. Where we talk of 'trainees', we will be explicitly talking about those who are training to achieve the title 'forensic psychologist'. Once registered with the HCPC, there is a formal requirement to continue to meet the relevant standards, often through attendance at continuing professional development programmes or through other developmental activities. As with all psychology professions, forensic psychologists keep learning and developing throughout their careers.

We've mentioned the BPS and the HCPC and will continue to do so throughout this book – but who are they?

In short, the BPS is the professional body for psychologists of all grades and is responsible for accrediting all academic programmes (undergraduate, MSc and professional doctorate programmes in forensic psychology) as well as offering the qualification of 'Chartered Status' to psychologists. The HCPC is the regulatory body for practitioner (registered) psychologists, which means that any issues of practice – whether it is fitness to practice, complaints or registration and authority to act as a practitioner psychologist – are handled by the HCPC. You *must* be registered with the HCPC and adhere to the code of conduct and ethical practice proscribed by the HCPC to practise as a forensic psychologist. If you get into trouble for any issues of practice, the HCPC will be the body which sanctions you!

What Does a Forensic Psychologist Do and Where?

So, what does a forensic psychologist do, and where are they employed?

Let us start with dispelling a myth first. Lots of people might think we just work with the 'mad' or the 'bad'. But it is much more complicated than that and hopefully, you will learn that those are not useful or appropriate descriptions of the people we work with – whether that is our client base or our colleagues! In fact, forensic psychologists work with a wide range of people, in a variety of settings. Amongst the reasons those 'mad or bad' terms are not useful is that it makes it much easier for people to think that those who are responsible for offending against society are either 'mad' or 'bad' and therefore not like the rest of us, so we don't need to worry or think about it or them. This is a bit of a tabloid mentality designed to try and make us feel better about ourselves and the world in which we live – if we think those people are so far removed from 'normal' society or people like us that they must be 'mad' or 'bad', then we do not need to assume any responsibility. In fact, we should really start thinking about ourselves and our society and hold a mirror up to our world to better understand that offenders are offending *within* our society and not outside of it. And once we think about things in that way, it opens the approach, attitude and range of work forensic psychologists are involved in. Mainly, we tend to operate within a 'legal' or 'criminal justice' type setting and the detail of what we do will depend upon where we work and the jurisdiction, legislation and aims of the relevant setting.

We'd also like to start by saying we will regularly use the term 'offenders' in this book. This is not a term that we prefer, but given the scope of the book and the range of settings in which people are held or managed, it becomes the 'easiest' nomenclature to use. But think about it as we use it, is someone in hospital who has been found not to have the capacity to stand trial as an offender? Is someone on licence who is no longer offending, an offender? What does this label mean when we apply it both to the individual it is being used with and to how we and others think about that person?

But to start with the most common settings forensic psychologists work – they include:

- Prisons
- Secure mental health units
- Community forensic mental health teams
- Private hospitals
- Universities
- Courts
- Probation Services
- Youth offending teams
- Police

Each of these settings has a different need for the forensic psychologist; at the court, it might be to make a decision around someone's fitness to plead or their ability to give evidence or be a credible witness, as well as offering up an explanation of 'why' the alleged offender did what they did, if it was preventable and what might be recommended for their rehabilitation to protect them and the public. Forensic psychology in a mental health setting has a different focus, as does that in a prison or a community setting. The core psychology remains the same, but the jurisdictions are different, as well as the relevant legal processes and the aimed-for outcomes. On a very basic level, the 'client' for the forensic psychologist may be the individual service user or might be a range of other stakeholders. This will depend on the setting and may vary within settings by the service being provided. This multiple-client context is important for forensic psychologists as, unlike many other domains of psychology, 'who the "client" is', is often rather complicated. For example, if the forensic psychologist is working as an 'expert', the stakeholders might include the offender (or alleged offender), the court, the public, the instructing solicitor(s) and the Parole Board to name just a few. This means the role has to be diverse, transparent and evidence-based so the decisions are defensible – and it does mean that there is rarely a dull day!

As to what we do, the four headings used within the BPS's qualification in forensic psychology[i] (QFP) provide a decent, if broad-brush, overview of the work, irrespective of the setting. These are:

- *Conducting applications and interventions*
- *Research*
- *Communicating with other professionals*
- *Training other professionals*

In practice, these can also be termed:

- *Assessment and intervention*
- *Research*
- *Consultancy*
- *Training*

These four main areas of work describe the specialist and varied work of a forensic psychologist, though some individuals will do more in one area than another, depending on the setting, their skills and preferences and their need.

The National Careers Service (nationalcareersservice.direct.gov.uk) provides an overview of the type of work a forensic psychologist might do, and all of it sounds pretty exciting:

- *Support police investigations through criminal profiling*
- *Support prison staff and other professionals in the welfare or criminal and civil justice systems working within criminal and civil justice or the welfare systems*
- *Carry out research to improve and develop professional practice*

A forensic psychologist would also work directly with offenders to help them understand and overcome their problems and behaviour patterns. You may:

- *Prepare risk assessments for offenders*
- *Advise on the best location for prisoners*
- *Develop treatment and rehabilitation programmes*
- *Provide psychological therapy*
- *Offer expert advice to Parole Boards, mental health tribunals or courts*
- *Produce formal written reports*
- *Help to write policies and strategies*
- *Train and mentor new psychologists*
- *Find ways to reduce stress and improve life inside prisons*

(nationalcareers.service.gov.uk/job-profiles/
forensic-psychologist)

This is a good overview of the role and the work involved. However, as with many forensic psychology descriptions, there is a tendency to focus more on the prison side of forensic psychology practice, possibly because historically that is where forensic psychologists have been based. Health settings tend to feature more clinical psychologists who also have a forensic specialism although within psychology things are changing with significantly higher numbers of forensic psychologists working in what has been predominantly a clinical psychology setting. There are also career opportunities working with forensic mental health in settings which include not only secure inpatient units but also community settings. Forensic psychologists are also able to apply their transferable skills gained through training in more diverse areas of safeguarding, policy, risk management, project management and innovatively developing new services for vulnerable and/or risky populations.

It is worth unpicking the National Careers website description in a little more detail. In terms of reducing stress and improving life in prisons, it is the case that forensic psychologists within the prison system are involved in activities to help shape regimes or contribute to a range of research or other activities aimed at, for example, reducing violence and improving well-being whilst in custody. It is this type of activity that tends to be termed 'consultancy'. Consultancy and research often go hand in hand, sometimes identifying and leading to 'training and development' as an identified outcome. Overall, the career descriptions provided are a little out of date and too prison-centric for the more modern-day practice of forensic psychology. From a review of other descriptions offered, this seems to be a common issue.

We mentioned earlier that the historical dominance of clinical psychology in health settings is starting to change, and this relates to forensic psychology, as our understanding of offender populations is also changing. The BPS has been promoting a 'recruitment by competence' approach to all employers. This basically means that psychologists should consider themselves to be skilled and specialised applied psychologists who can deliver services in a variety of settings, recognising the existence and importance of core transferable skills. Psychologists should consider themselves as able to work in lots of places with the analytical skills acquired through training, development and wider practice. Within health and criminal justice, this includes the community – with Probation Services, charities and the voluntary sector, the health services and prisons. But once you develop your skills as a manager, supervisor, scientist and practitioner, then you might find you can apply these skills to a variety of other services. This allows a degree of creativity within the profession and poses a question to qualified forensic psychologists – what skills do you think you have acquired, and how else could they be utilised? If you consider the training requirements outlined above, you can see that having an analytical and organised approach to understanding volumes of complex information, adopting skills of project management and understanding stress and the impact of environments and other triggers upon behaviour, along with understanding how to determine the outcomes from patterns of behaviour and activity, are just some of the skills a forensic psychologist develops, which can be applied to a number of roles – in psychological and non-psychological professions.

Notwithstanding the transferable skills you will gain through the process of training and qualification, it is important to be aware of the typical settings in which you are most likely to work as a forensic psychologist. We have touched on some of this earlier but will focus now on the main areas.

His Majesty's Prison and Probation Service (HMPPS)

HMPPS is responsible for the employment of forensic psychologists and trainee forensic psychologists in a range of roles across the HM Prison Service, the Probation Service and the HMPPS HQ. It is the largest single employer of this group of professionals and hence can provide a wider range of information about forensic psychology staff, work and standards given the centrally held nature of the records.

The work of a forensic psychologist for HMPPS can vary depending on grade, location and local need, but broadly the areas of work are as follows:

Offender management processes: Forensic psychologists complete a range of assessments that feed into the offender management process within HMPPS. This may be linked to sentence planning for those convicted of an indeterminate sentence or reporting on an individual's risk of reoffending directly to the Parole Board who are considering whether a prisoner is sufficiently low risk to justify release into the community on licence.[3] It might be reporting to internal sentence planning boards, for example in relation to categorisation[ii] or linked with wider assessments and formulation for the offending behaviour programmes (OBPs) which we will cover later. Forensic psychologists provide advice and guidance and direct case input to those deemed at risk of harm to themselves or to others in custody, as well as on release. This involves lots of face-to-face work with prisoners, focusing on risk and rehabilitation. It is important to note that often the media, and also academic papers, may use the term 'offenders'[iii] or 'prisoners' rather pejoratively. However, we prefer not to think of 'them and us'. Rather, we think about those we work with first and foremost as people who, like any of us, might have a slightly different background and their own set of experiences, sometimes traumatic or difficult, or who sometimes have a different way of seeing and experiencing the world and putting their thoughts together, which has led to a difficult outcome. This helps us to do the best job we can as forensic psychologists – whether it is assessing, treating, teaching, training or consultancy.

Interventions: Forensic psychologists within HMPPS will work on both delivering and 'treatment managing' high-intensity OBPs with prisoners. Some of these are delivered in a small group setting and some on a 1–1 basis. 'Treatment management' is a term used to describe providing the clinical/quality oversight of the OBP to ensure that those facilitating the group do so appropriately, as well as ensuring that the selection of prisoners for the group and their progress throughout the OBP are well managed. Some believe that OBPs are overly 'manualised', leaving insufficient flexibility for the practitioner to provide the individual approach that a prisoner may need. Others feel that OBPs are an 'experiment' that has not yet shown sufficient impact on reducing reoffending to justify their delivery or expense. Yet more regard OBPs as one of a range of approaches that can be offered to prisoners to assist in reducing their reoffending whilst recognising they are no magic bullet and a whole range of other changes are needed, either by the prisoners themselves or linked to other factors such as availability of accommodation or employment on release. This is a big debate within forensic psychology and has been ongoing for some time. You will see a number of references for further reading, which will help you make up your own mind. Suffice it to say that there is a defensible argument that OBPs within HMPPS are evidence-informed and are updated regularly following consultation with a range of international experts.

In addition to these accredited OBPs, psychologists provide individual intervention; this may be because individuals are not best suited to mainstream OBPs due to, for example, learning difficulties, or it might be because mainstream programmes do not exist, or there is a need to focus on a particular issue. The key to thinking about helping people change is understanding that 'formulation' is the key. This means understanding 'what's going on and why' for a person. As the poet John Donne said, *'no man is an island'*, and this is a key principle for forensic psychologists and how you can begin to develop ideas of change and interventions. People do not tend to act alone in a closed system, and the role of the forensic psychologist is to understand what influences behaviour or actions – including the person's relationship with others, their environment, personality and any response to traumas they might have experienced. Forensic psychologists work with people who have often done bad things but often they have experienced bad things themselves, and it might not be fair to 'judge' a person based only on the worst thing they have ever done. We would argue there is more to a person than that – after all, would you like to be 'judged' on the worst thing you have done? The role of a forensic psychologist is vital in understanding the why, how, what risk and what intervention or strategy to prevent a future bad outcome might be required.

Forensic psychologists also work in a range of specialist custodial settings including therapeutic communities,[iv] psychologically informed and planned environments (PIPEs),[v] and other units aimed at working with specific prison populations. Here, they provide a range of direct services and consultancy support to prisoners and staff.[vi]

Away from the prisoner-facing work, forensic psychologists provide a range of research and training in areas where psychological skills and expertise are either required or best practices. An example would be training prison officers to be negotiators; such staff have a specific role during prison incident management procedures. Research may relate to fairly simple impact assessments of changes to a prison system or policy, through to more formal research and evaluation into any number of areas. Prison governors and other staff groups may need advice or support to develop strategies which draw upon psychological knowledge. For example, the factors associated with developing an enabling and rehabilitative culture.

Outside of prisons, there are currently a low number of forensic psychologists directly employed by HMPPS to work in the community, and their roles therefore take on a greater consultancy support element for the community offender managers (probation officers) whom they work with. Hence, these roles tend to focus on providing specialist advice and guidance on working with high-risk cases. Because of the large number of offenders under the remit of the Probation Service (PS), only a relatively limited amount of 'hands-on' assessment or intervention is possible in this setting. We understand that this remains under review, as, of course, in the community, those under licence conditions or community sentences have access to other services as would any citizen.

Thus, other forensic psychology services are drawn from other sectors in the community – including the voluntary sector, charities or the NHS. This is discussed in more depth later in this book, but it is important to remember that it is possible for you to be creative in the workplace, to seek to deploy your skills outside of a traditional employment framework and even look to develop your own unique service provision. This tends to happen later in your career, once you are fully qualified and have some experience of working in the field. It is as much about being credible and having the experience to back up your ideas or your proposal. You need to be able to communicate the skills, experience and value you offer from your own training, working history and experiences. Forensic psychology does offer you an opportunity to develop your thinking and your skills should you choose to embrace it. What we're trying to say is that forensic psychology is a sufficiently wide sphere that you can work through a variety of employers to work with different client groups depending on your skills and the needs of the service users/agencies.

Forensic psychologists are also employed by HMPPS at a national level in a range of roles. This includes, in evidence and research teams, reviewing the knowledge base and making recommendations for future services and regimes. It also includes those who develop the aforementioned OBPs and retain a clinical responsibility for them at a national level and those who work with other policy groups, such as in security, safety or the women's team, assisting with policy development across the service.

The Police Service

Forensic psychologists may be directly employed by the police to assist with a range of work, or they may be brought in on a more private consultancy basis for specific tasks.

This work may include assisting in developing skills in the workforce in relation to crisis negotiation and working as a consultant in assessing an individual's ability to undergo questioning or indeed how best to question based on the person's characteristics. This more investigative approach is easily sensationalised and turned into books or TV programmes, but there is some truth to it. For example, Dr Julian Boon is a forensic psychologist based at the University of Leicester who has been professionally engaged in this type of work over the years and has published widely, so it's worth giving him a Google.

Whilst the type of 'forensic psychology' you see on TV has undoubtedly popularised the subject and made it more accessible to the mainstream, as a science, forensic psychology has also become more widely recognised – particularly in the last couple of decades, there is increased coverage of forensic psychology in academic settings, in both teaching and research. The popular TV and film focus on forensic psychology, alongside a seemingly insatiable appetite for books about crime, has led to an increase in both undergraduate and postgraduate courses offering specialist coverage of forensic psychology. This has increased the range of opportunities for forensic psychologists to work within university and higher education settings, teaching and training others. Posts within universities also provide a range of opportunities for academic research with notable specialist research teams around the country.

Youth Offending Teams (YOTs)

Youth offending teams work with young people under the age of 18. YOTs are part of the local council arrangements and are separate from the police and the courts. They are overseen by the Youth Justice Board (YJB), who also oversee custodial placements for under-18s within HMPPS and other secure settings. They work with a range of agencies (e.g. schools, health and children's services) and aim to help young people who get into trouble with the law to stay away from crime and get further involved in offending.

The involvement of psychology in these teams can be a mix of domains, with educational, clinical, counselling and forensic being the most common. Each domain brings something slightly different to the team. Indeed, some YOTs use only educational services.

Forensic psychologists in this setting largely carry out assessment and intervention work as well as provide support and consultancy advice to the YOT workers assigned to an individual. The balance of work will depend on the level of resources available and the size of the caseload.

Mental Health Settings

Firstly, what do we mean by a mental health setting?

Forensic mental health services are provided for those who experience mental distress and who might have received a formal psychiatric diagnosis. Some psychologists question the value of the psychiatric diagnostic approach, but in the current system, those who might meet the criteria for diagnosis of a mental disorder and who pose (or have posed) risks to others, (usually where the risk is related to the mental disorder) may fall under the specialist remit of a forensic psychologist working in mental health. This reflects the broadening scope of activity for forensic psychologists and the settings in which they can work. These include:

- Special hospitals
- Prison-based units
- Medium secure units
- Low secure units
- Community settings
- Court/custody liaison and diversion services

Historically, where the consideration has been mental health, the settings have tended to focus the psychology workforce on clinical psychology. However, as our understanding of mental distress, trauma and other influencing variables on antisocial behaviours has developed, so has the role of forensic psychologists working in this area. Understanding the role of mental well-being, mental distress or presenting patterns of mental illness has become crucial in our understanding of risk, intervention and prevention, so forensic psychologists are increasingly utilised in this field – in both public and private health settings. We would recommend reading around the power threat meaning framework as a counter to the psychiatric diagnostic approach.[4]

Private Work

Given the demand for forensic psychology services, some individuals choose to work privately, often setting up their own company. They might then be commissioned by solicitors on behalf of prisoners to write reports for the Parole Board. These reports are described as 'independent' because they are not written by an individual employed by the

Prison Service. Others regard such reports as less 'independent' because the prisoner can choose not to disclose a privately commissioned report to the Parole Board should they wish to. There is a wealth of private work available both to supplement directly employed workforces and as part of court reporting in a variety of settings. For example, the family court often tends to use forensic psychologists, and yet, this is often an overlooked area of practice. Others provide expert testimony to courts at different stages of an individual's trial and sentencing, sometimes following initial work on a case with the police.

Within family courts, the role of a forensic psychologist can be very challenging. It has been said that the most draconian thing a state can do to a person short of the death penalty is to remove their child for permanent adoption. A forensic psychologist often has a key role in the court's decision to remove a child from its parent/parents. The psychological risk assessment prepared as an expert report is likely to be a key factor informing all parties – from social services, the independent children's guardian and the court itself, of the possible risks the child might be exposed to and whether the parent(s) can effect change in a reasonable time to offer that child a safe and stable upbringing. It is a very difficult line of work and fraught with emotion on all sides, so it is not for the faint-hearted.

A core activity in all of the settings and different posts described for a forensic psychologist is being called upon to provide expert witness testimony.

Often, a forensic psychologist can be called on to offer advice and opinions to a court in an expert capacity. Forensic psychologists are often described as 'experts' and indeed can be employed to provide expert assessment reports and give evidence in court as expert witnesses. This can be in civil/family courts (as described above) and often in criminal cases – as an expert identified to provide a professional, evidence-based opinion on risk, mental disorder, cognitive functioning, personality factors or treatability. This can take place during a trial where, as in civil cases, the forensic psychologist as an expert is subject to cross-examination by two or more barristers. The expertise can also be used at the point of sentencing to advise or assist the court on possible sentencing disposals. There is a distinction to be drawn between an expert witness and a professional witness, and the BPS has produced some helpful guidelines which can be downloaded for free, explaining the role and function of the psychologist as an expert witness (www. bps.org.uk/guideline/psychologists-expert-witnesses).

The Client Group

So, there are a range of settings, but who are the people with whom forensic psychologists work?

If you are applying for a place at a university or a job, it is worth thinking about the various challenges of working with various groups and in various settings. So, for example – consider what the specific problems might be in working with a young male population. What difficulties might they pose? What difficulties might you have to address as a result of your own gender, social background or any other personal factor? How might you manage this effectively? What might be the effect or impact of the environment or context on your ability to carry out your duties effectively? Beginning to think along these lines across the different client groups is beginning to think like an effective and reflective practitioner.

In most settings, inevitably forensic psychologists are often working with complex individuals who on the whole, are not consenting to be part of the criminal justice or related health setting to which they are linked. This invariably raises issues in relation to informed consent and consideration of different ways of working with this client group. In the vast majority of cases, the reason a forensic psychologist is involved is that an individual either is at risk of entering the criminal justice system or is already in it whilst acknowledging that some placements into health settings are alternatives to prison custody. And often these individuals can be hard to engage, challenging or have a deliberate agenda to put across, which the forensic psychologist must be able to address and consider in their approach.

The types of cases that generally attract the services of a forensic psychologist are those deemed the most complex and those thought most likely to cause harm to themselves or others. This may be at any stage in the process, from police investigation to court to considering the most appropriate sentence or custodial/health placement (sometimes referred to as the 'disposal', although that word doesn't seem a particularly pleasant word to use!) or to working with individuals once held within different parts of the system. There are of course some exceptions to every rule. For example, some services are developing to help individuals cope or deal with issues before they become damaging. Indeed, there is at least one charity-led service where men who struggle with a sexual interest in children but who have never acted upon it, can receive support and intervention to help manage or reduce such interest.[5] Such schemes aim to protect potential victims and divert potential offenders from criminal and/or damaging behaviour.

The individuals you may work with will generally have committed serious offences. These offences may be violent, sexual or both. Alternatively, the presenting (index) offence may not be serious, but the behaviour and attitude of the individual are seen as problematic. They may or may not recognise their offending as an antisocial act. It is also likely that at some point you will work with individuals whose offences may be very hard for you to appropriately deal with personally. Some people want to get into forensic psychology work to focus on the 'serial killers' and the notoriety and 'excitement' of working with such people. If this is your interest, we would suggest you spend some time thinking about your career choice. Firstly, general forensic psychology is not like that. Secondly, an 'unhealthy' interest in notorious cases and some sense of glamour from knowing and working with such individuals might suggest that it would be helpful to reflect on your motivation for entering into this type of work, or at least which part of the forensic 'system', you may be best suited to.

As a forensic psychologist, you will be dealing with a wide range of people who have committed a range of offences. Excuse the use of the term 'offender' in this paragraph, and at other times throughout this book, but these may include young offenders, gang members, sexual offenders, internet sex offenders, violent offenders and women offenders. Within each of these groups, there will be individuals of varying ages and criminal records, offence types, with different personality types, levels of insight and acceptance of their situation. You will also experience different responses to you as the forensic psychologist. This can vary from open engagement to open hostility based on previous experience or beliefs about the profession, or confusion as to your role compared to other psychologists they have worked with, perhaps, who had different confidentiality boundaries, which may not always be replicated in some forensic settings.

As in any role, there will also be some individuals who seek to manipulate and persuade you, given your perceived influence. And there will be others who have lost hope and who need support, motivation and care. The difference between a forensic psychologist employed by HMPPS and a forensic psychologist employed by a mental health service is not always obvious, particularly to offenders. This is why 'informed consent' is so important and must be very clearly explained and agreed upon before embarking on any work with individuals. We will say more about this later but broadly speaking psychologists directly employed by HMPPS are there to work alongside prisoners as part of a wider system which seeks to protect against further victimisation. This means that the information provided is not confidential, although it is handled with care and shared only as necessary, but is part of sentence planning and reporting. Within health settings, information is regarded as 'medical in-confidence' and handled differently. This must be made clear to individual prisoners, or else they may believe levels of confidentiality, which are not available to the HMPPS employee, and they may be providing consent to engage in a process without understanding how their information is going to be managed and shared. The area of consent and confidentiality can be complex to understand but as a very general rule, for the practising forensic psychologist, it is often impossible to offer complete confidentiality, as any information we would consider to be 'relevant to risk' can and should be shared with appropriate individuals or agencies. Sometimes, there is no confidentiality at all (e.g. if you are assessing someone for the purpose of a court report), and so context and informed consent are especially important to understand and communicate for the ethical practitioner psychologist.

It is possible to specialise once qualified if you have a particular area of interest or expertise, but in your training years you should be prepared to work with as many client groups as possible in order to gain a breadth and depth of experience and knowledge. You will probably prefer some client groups more than others and will therefore be more effective at working with them. Knowing your skill set and the impact you can have is an important piece of insight for any psychologist, not just a forensic psychologist. It is also highly likely that the impact of your own skill or knowledge limitations or biases will have an even greater impact on those incarcerated against their will, given the opportunity for a power imbalance. It becomes your duty to do the best possible job you can do, with the best available information, using the best of your ability. And this duty extends not only to the 'client' but also to wider society. So, operating within your specialism and within your competencies along with principles of sound evidence-based practice as a scientist-practitioner should underpin every aspect of how you work and who you work with.

It is therefore important to consider each of these offender groups in a little more detail.

Young Offenders (Also Historically Sometimes Referred to as 'Juvenile' Offenders)[vii]

Firstly, a little context.

- We know that those who start their offending earlier are more likely to persist in their offending
- Not all offence types 'persist' in the same way
- We know that the prevalence of offending tends to increase from late childhood, peak in the late teen years and then decline in the early 20s. This is known as the age – crime curve, which is a universal finding in western populations (see Loeber & Farrington, 2014)
- We know the age – crime curve is different for boys/girls and for different offence types

Most in this group are male, though there has been an increase in the number of girls in recent years. The main offences committed by young males are theft, handling stolen goods, violence against the person and criminal damage, though there appears to be a growing number who are committing more serious offences – these may include serious assault, murder, rape and sexual offences against children. As a consequence, there is a growing population of young males serving custodial sentences, and this can present quite specific problems in terms of managing and attempting to help them change their behaviour.

Given that we know that many young offenders desist, psychologists can focus on supporting those who will 'naturally' desist whilst focusing more targeted interventions on those who are more likely to go on to persist in their offending behaviour.

Young people, or in fact children, detained through the criminal justice system are located in three main settings, all overseen by the Youth Justice Board (YJB), and may encounter forensic psychologists in any of these:

- Secure children's homes (SCHs): There are currently 15 individually managed SCHs run by local councils in England and Wales. They provide placements for boys and girls aged between 10 and 14, providing residential care, educational facilities and healthcare provision
- Secure training centres: Run by private companies, they hold boys and girls up to 17 years old
- Prisons for young people: Run by the HMPPS and private companies for those aged 15 to 18. They have held only boys for several years but, at the time of writing, also hold a very small number of girls

The decision as to which type of setting an individual may be located in will depend on their offence, their past history and the risk they present.

There are several psychological theories that attempt to explain crime within this age group. These include cognitive theories which suggest that young people who offend think differently from non-offenders, with the relationship between intelligence and criminal behaviour a recurring feature.

These findings, however, should be tempered by the fact that low 'intelligence quotient' or IQ scores may simply reflect social disadvantage rather than intellectual ability. It is also important to note that our understanding of cognitive functioning and the conceptualisation of intellectual ability has moved on considerably in recent years, and making conclusions about an individual based on their full-scale IQ scores is open to considerable challenge. Now, we would consider intellectual functioning more holistically, including how an individual processes and retains information and their ability to learn.

Ross and Fabiano (1985) argued that different cognitive styles might be associated with offending. These styles include self-control, locus of control, perspective taking, moral development and social problem-solving. Several intervention approaches have been designed to specifically address these cognitive traits.

Bandura (1977; Bandura & National Inst. of Mental Health, 1986) developed social learning theory, suggesting that behaviour can be learnt at a cognitive level by observing others' behaviour and then performing likewise when it is likely to be reinforced by peers.

Moral development theory suggests that our behaviour is related to the way we think and reason. Kohlberg (1976) described three levels of moral development in children:

- *Pre-conventional level* (when the individual considers obedience on the basis of likely punishment against what might be in it for them)
- *Conventional level* (when the individual considers social norms and obeys rules in order to be 'a good boy/girl' and live up to expectations)
- *Post-conventional level* (when the individual understands the rules of society and the principles underlying them)

Gibbs et al. (1992) suggest, based on their evaluation of Kohlberg's theories, a potential link between delinquency and lower levels of moral reasoning, whilst Eisenberg and Mussen (1989) found that in a number of studies, low levels of moral reasoning predicted delinquency and dishonesty. Loeber et al. (1993) suggest three potential pathways to delinquency – overt, covert and authority conflict pathways:

- The *overt pathway* in which behaviour that begins as minor aggressive behaviour, such as bullying, then intensifies, leading to more violent behaviour, such as fighting, and ultimately escalates to offences such as assault, robbery or rape
- The *covert pathway* in which behaviour escalates from lying and vandalism to more serious acts of theft and damage, such as arson
- The *authority conflict pathway*, which begins with minor disobedience and escalates to truanting and running away

A young person may follow more than one pathway, in which case there is an even higher probability of offending behaviour.

Moffitt (1993) found that temporary and situational antisocial behaviour is relatively common in young adolescents and suggests that there are two types of offender – *adolescent-limited* and *life-course-persistent* offenders. The first group typically begins offending during adolescence and then desists when entering early adulthood, whereas life-course-persistent offenders begin offending early and then continue this pattern. Another finding was that 5% of this sample showed antisocial behaviour before starting school, and 33% who had not previously shown antisocial behaviour began to get involved in offending between the ages of 11 and 15. This group tended to show a decrease in their offending as they got older, whereas the early starters were more likely to continue offending.

All of this theory must be understood in order to effectively engage with this age group. Forensic psychologists can be involved in carrying out assessments of young people through the previously mentioned YOTs and once in a secure setting in order to assess the likelihood of reoffending. This may determine sentence plans, interventions[viii] and release preparations and can involve a range of assessments which may also include a measure of cognitive functioning or the risk of self-harm and suicide. However, many assessment measures are developed for adults and are unsuitable for those in this age group who may be offending. This means we have to be careful with our approach to assessing young people and adapt the way we conduct ourselves, the gathering of information and the tests we use. Care must be taken when identifying measures to use as their validity can be questionable,[6] and we must be mindful of a variety of possibly influencing variables including any intellectual functioning or learning difficulties, attention or concentration problems, and of course, it is not unusual for a young person to have next to no desire to engage with an apparently old or seemingly ancient psychologist, so issues around motivation must be addressed.

Both individual and group programmes can be effective when working with young people. Those which appear to be the most effective in terms of reducing reoffending tend to focus on interpersonal skills training, individual structured counselling and offending behaviour programmes. Individual work with offenders can also complement progress in group work, especially if the principles of risk and need guide interventions.[7] However, low motivation for offenders to change can present challenges, and these feelings need to be explored sensitively in order for individuals to feel able to effectively engage with any assessments or interventions. A key skill for an effective practitioner is building rapport, but this needs to be done sensitively and over time, with the aim to be collaborative, encouraging and empowering. There is also a need to be realistic and to prepare for challenges along the way.

Thus, forensic psychologists working with children and young people need to be aware of the young people's specific literature and engage and tailor their practice to best meet the needs and demands of this group.

Those Convicted of Sexual Offences

Members of this group can often be some of the most challenging and complex clients for forensic psychologists. The group includes male and female offenders, adults and young people. Offences may be 'contact' or 'non-contact' (e.g. internet-based) or may include levels of child exploitation.[8]

There are a number of theories and models around sexual offending. You may want to read Finkelhor (1984), who was one of the first authors to present a model of child sexual abuse and proposed four necessary steps or preconditions for abuse to occur. We have Hall and Hirschman (1992) with their Quadripartite Model which includes four preconditions. Or Ward and Siegert (2002), who produced a Pathways Model that provides a comprehensive review of the range of different theories that try to explain sexual offending. We could go on! Theories of sexual offending abound as there are a range of different sexual behaviours which are criminal. Some are sexually motivated, and some are more driven by power. However, these different models all have a number of common features that include:

- Dysfunctional schemas and distorted beliefs
- Attachment and interpersonal problems
- Deviant sexual arousal and distorted sexual scripts
- Difficulties in regulating emotional states

As a forensic psychologist working with this client group, we need to understand the theories and be able to apply our knowledge to individual clients to best understand their offending behaviour and work with them to reduce their risk.

Internet sex offenders present a more recent challenge in terms of assessment and treatment. The term refers to those convicted of 'accessing, downloading and possessing indecent images or pseudo-images which depict the sexual abuse of children' (Middleton et al., 2006). One response to this offending type has been the setting-up of the Internet Sexual Offences Treatment Programme (i-SOTP, Middleton et al., 2009). This programme was designed to be delivered in the community in either individual or group format, though those offenders deemed to be 'very high risk' of reoffending might be expected to complete a more intensive intervention. The i-SOTP was developed by combining the 'model of change' from previous accredited OBPs and the Good Lives Model.[9]

A range of settings, both secure and community-based, provides treatment approaches for sexual offenders. Success, however, can be difficult to measure, as recorded reoffending rates tend to be low for this offence type, making change difficult to measure (Mews et al., 2017). The role of the forensic psychologist with this population – like any other – is to understand the factors or pathways which led to the offending behaviour, the motivation, the nature of the offence and the psychology of the perpetrator. These can include a wide variety of factors, including possibly their own experience of being abused and the sometimes cyclical relationship between victim and perpetrator. The theories around sexual offending and our understanding of these types of offences are developing all the time and it is important for the forensic psychologist to divorce themselves from the mainstream and media presentations of these types of offences to try and understand and work with the people behind them. For some this is a difficult ethical process and there is no doubt that some very difficult offence stories, victim impact statements and consequences of the behaviour will have to be addressed by the forensic psychologist working in this area – both professionally and personally. This is where understanding the theory as well as the wider cultural perspective places forensic psychologists at the front line of challenging moral, societal and media issues. Theories can assist us in understanding the heterogeneity of this cohort of offenders (should an adult 'date-rapist' as the media like to label people, for example, be considered in the same category as a manipulative abuser of children?),[ix] but working with this client group also points to the role a forensic psychologist can play in informing public debate and discourse with necessary communication of the nuances and complexity of risk assessment, particularly given the media portrayal of offending.

Women Offenders

It is unquestionable that women offenders present a significantly smaller proportion of the offender population (around 4–5% of the prison population), but only relatively recently has there been proper recognition that this group needs gender-specific services. Historically, there has been more limited research on women offenders and consequently limited exploration of what might constitute appropriate treatment and detention of women offenders within forensic settings.

Whilst there are numerous theories that attempt to explain offending by women, it is the 'generalisability problem' that has dominated thinking in this area. This problem concerns the tendency of general theories of crime to assume that the same theories of crime can apply equally to both men and women. This subsequently led to an increase in what was called 'feminist criminology',[10] which explored potential links between female crime and mental illness. More recently, theories of crime have moved away from a feminist perspective towards a more global theory of offending by women, acknowledging similarities to, as well as differences from, male offenders.

Early studies of women offenders had highlighted the tendency for the criminal activity of these individuals to have arisen within a context of the involvement in the crime of family members and friends and the presence of domestic violence (Chesney-Lind, 1997). Interestingly, criminologists have either shown little interest in women and crime or reached the conclusion that such women should be seen as 'mad' rather than 'bad' (Bottoms, 1996). Similarly, Broidy and Agnew (1997) identify major differences between men and women in their response to strain. For instance, women are described as being more likely to respond with depression, whilst men are described as being more likely to respond with anger. Similarly, whilst men are described as 'quick to blame others and less concerned about hurting others', women are described as 'more likely to blame themselves and worry about the effects of their anger'. Such differences are, of course, important in designing and delivering services.

It has been a common finding that women offenders may have a history of abuse and possible associated feelings of self-loathing. Briere and Runtz (1988) suggest that traumatised people may develop destructive patterns of behaviour, which can include self-mutilation and drug and alcohol abuse and this is a significant feature associated with female offenders, which will require attention and treatment. Women offenders may establish a protective persona to present to those in authority and thus keep them at a distance, and it may therefore take some time to establish sufficient trust to enable intervention strategies to be effective.[11]

Without doubt, the women offender population merits more attention and research and should not be considered as merely an offender group with slightly different needs from the larger group of male offenders. Over recent years in custody, there has been an increased interest and understanding of the importance of trauma-based approaches to improving the care and engagement of women offenders.

If interested in this client group, we recommend you read the 2007 Corston Report.[12]

Gangs

Criminal gangs are not a new phenomenon, although it has been suggested that the rise of immigration and population levels, the availability of vehicles and lethal weapons and the growing involvement of some street gangs in illegal drug markets may have contributed to increasing levels of gang membership. Becoming a gang member can also provide a degree of protection in a community where there is gang rivalry. Early theorists suggested that economic destabilisation, combined with social disorganisation, often leads to a breakdown in family life, which in turn leads youngsters to seek both excitement and protection elsewhere. Gang membership may be seen as an attractive alternative to conventional norms whilst also providing a social structure. Psychological explanations have also been proffered, such as delinquency being the outcome of early childhood maldevelopment, such as separation or having unhealthy role models.

Forensic psychologists may be involved in the assessment and subsequent intervention with those within gangs or who have strong identities which link with offending behaviour. Increasingly, we are seeing that forensic psychologists involved in research are becoming involved in multidisciplinary research in this area, including psychologists from a wide range of specialisms, social anthropologists, criminologists, social policy and many other areas. The practical and theoretical work of forensic psychologists is a key component in understanding and forwarding theories around gangs and how we work with those who have become involved with such a subculture. Understanding the nature of fear and reward, group adhesion, commitment and value are just some of the areas we might explore in our work with gangs.

Extremist Offenders

'Extremism' and 'radicalisation' are terms that have entered our vocabulary more in recent years than before. In this section, it may be useful to begin with some definitions.

Extremism

The promotion or advancement of an ideology based on violence, hatred or intolerance that aims to:

negate or destroy the fundamental rights and freedoms of others; or
undermine, overturn or replace the UK's system of liberal parliamentary democracy and democratic rights; or
intentionally create a permissive environment for others to achieve the results in (1) or (2).

Extremist offenders: These are those whose offences are committed in association with a group, cause or ideology that propagates extremist views and actions and justifies the use of violence and other illegal activities in pursuit of its objectives.
Radicalisation: The process by which a person comes to support terrorism and extremist ideologies associated with terrorist groups.
Violent extremism: Extremism accompanied by violence.
Terrorism: An action that endangers or causes serious violence to a person/people; causes serious damage to property; or seriously interferes with or disrupts an electronic system. The use of threat must be designed to influence the government or to intimidate the

public and is made for the purpose of advancing a political, religious or ideological cause (Terrorism Act 2000).

Terrorism-related offences: These are those (such as murder) which are not offences in terrorist legislation but which are judged by HMPPS to have been committed in relation to terrorism.

Extreme and radical thinking and the radicalisation of others, or attempts to, can be traced historically not just over decades but over centuries. There are examples of this found through historical texts covering the time over which history is recorded. In short, extremism, radicalisation and terrorism are not new phenomena despite being more in the popular conscience than before. Forensic psychologists have been at the forefront of developing risk assessments and in forming policy at a wider governmental level. This section includes the approaches taken by the Division of Forensic Psychology policy stream dedicated to extremism and is indicative of the expanding role forensic psychologists play in potentially controversial areas of policy.

The development and growth of so-called Islamist extremism and radicalisation can be mapped historically. That we are currently in a period where there is significant unrest, threat and resistance by and towards Islamist extremists is evident, and that this situation is of global importance and potentially influencing future history is also evident. Whilst this group has the most media coverage and arguably is the most influential, there are other extremist groups which also present a threat to others, all of which sit under the broad umbrella of extremism, radicalisation and terrorism. Psychology has a significant and important role to play on a number of levels in relation to this area, and it is important that this role is steered by the professional body and that this body has a role in equipping and guiding practice and wider policy.

The BPS has, in the past, attempted, through the development and considered deliberations of a working party, to develop policy in relation to this area of work.

In recent years, the DFP identified a number of policy 'strands' where the Division felt there needed to be a greater, more considered and more integrated focus and where the ultimate objective would be to influence, inform or advise others including policymakers and/or developers. One of these policy strands was 'extremism/radicalisation'. The strategic aims and objectives of the policy stream were identified as below. These are useful to understand as they outline the role of forensic psychology in this area of work. As a result, the DFP produced a guide to working in this area, and this can be downloaded for free:

www.bps.org.uk/guideline/ethical-guidelines-applied-psychological-
    practice-field-extremism-violent-extremism-and-0

Forensic psychologists work with individuals convicted of or suspected of offending related to their extremist beliefs to understand the risk they pose and seek to reduce that risk. This is an area of controversy in forensic psychology but also one that seems unlikely to go away.

Violent Offenders

Working with this group can be challenging and is often confused with the idea of working with 'anger'. Angry people can be violent, but you do not need to be angry to be violent and, of course, not all angry people act violently.

Novaco (1994) describes anger as a subjective emotional state, which is defined by the presence of physiological arousal and antagonistic thoughts. Aggression, meanwhile, is an overt behaviour (physical or verbal) that brings harm (or the potential of harm) to another person, object or system. Hollin and Howell (1989) describe aggression as 'the intention to hurt or gain advantage over other people, without necessarily involving physical injury'. Violence can be defined as those acts in which there is a deliberate attempt to inflict physical harm and can overlap with aggression.

Working with violent individuals is a core part of most forensic psychology client work. But what is it like working with this group? Well, in truth, it is much like working with anyone else! We are dealing with people who have a problem, which is impacting both themselves and others.

Understanding the theory and bringing it into practice are essential to help us place a framework around our thinking, utilise appropriate structured risk assessment and psychometric measures (e.g. is anger a feature of the violence, and therefore, is an anger measure required? Is the violence domain specific as in intimate partner violence (IPV)?) and of course inform treatment – whether this is a group programme or a one-to-one approach. Programmes such as 'Life Minus Violence' aim to synthesise some of this thinking.

Some Presenting Issues: Responsivity

Amongst all of the above, people will also present with a range of other issues, which may include coexisting mental health and/or developmental issues. This may include previous trauma, post-traumatic stress disorder (PTSD), psychopathy, personality disorders, learning difficulties and challenges. All our work should identify such factors and seek to be responsive and tailored to the particular needs of the client group.

Multiple Clients

Forensic psychologists, perhaps more than other psychology domains, continually have a range of stakeholders or 'multiple clients'. To overly generalise for a moment, we sometimes describe this simply as, for clinical psychologists working within the health setting, the client is most often the person in the chair undergoing whatever assessment or therapy is identified. For forensic psychologists, the client is the person in the chair but also usually widened to the public, the Parole Board and the governor, to name but a few, depending on the setting in question. Of course, clinical and other psychologists do have other stakeholder clients with potentially different agendas, but we believe this is most acute in forensic settings outside of health remits. This continual balance of ethical practice and the rights and responsibilities of the client and the psychologist can at times be difficult. Forensic psychologists need to be aware of the potential for conflict and ensure they maintain clear and transparent communication with those engaged in a case as to their aims and their purpose. We mentioned informed consent previously; aspects of confidentiality and the purpose of the forensic psychologist to be focused on public protection and risk, not solely on an individual's psychological state, can be a difficult balance to achieve.

A Little About the Forensic Psychology Workforce

We've talked about the client or population types you may work with, but what about the professional group that you would become part of? It should be noted that the majority of forensic psychologists are women operating in male (often custodial) settings. This can present a number of potential issues worth considering. Firstly, male prisoners may see this group of practitioners as providing a rare opportunity for them to engage with women. Inevitably, this is likely to impact their behaviour and needs to be taken into account when preparing for and engaging in interviews. Secondly, older male prisoners (potentially from a different ethnic, cultural and socio-economic background) may find being 'assessed' by a young woman (often white) patronising. Psychologists need to be mindful of these dynamics. Work is progressing within the Division of Forensic Psychology to 'decolonise the profession'.

Central records are not readily available, but we have pieced together some data which should give you some idea.

Practitioner psychologists are those registered with the HCPC and eligible to use a protected title such as 'forensic psychologist'. The use of the protected title shows they have passed the necessary gateways to be regarded as 'qualified' and hence an independent practitioner in their field rather than being 'in training'.

The following table shows the number of forensic psychologists registered with the HCPC over time. The HCPC opened their psychology register in June 2009 and had a period of 'grandparenting' where those not already listed on the BPS register who were automatically

Table 2.1 HCPC data relating to forensic psychologists

Date	Total	Female	Male	Unlisted
September 2009	500	-	-	-
February 2012	631	515	116	0
October 2015	822	700	122	0
March 2019	1,091	951	140	0
July 2023	1,755	1,430	265	60

Source: Historical data come from a range of FoI on the HCPC website with the most recent data here: www.hcpc-uk.org/resources/data/2023/diversity-data-practitioner-psychologists-2023/

transferred over could apply to join. It is for that main reason that we see the growth in the first few years of operation of the register.

You may have noticed the 'slight' gender imbalance visible here in the forensic psychologist workforce! It's worth putting this into context.

In June 2018, there were 22,288 psychologists on the HCPC register; hence, forensic psychologists[x] were an estimated 4% of the practitioner population (given the June 18 and March 19 comparisons). Of that 22,288, we see 18,103 (81%) were recorded as female with 19% (4,178) male. An update for 2023, there are 27,085 psychologists on the HCPC register, 79% recorded as female and 17% as male.

So, we know that psychology as a profession is dominated by women with 79% of all registered psychologists. In forensic psychology, this is marginally higher at 81%, although it has been as high as an 87% female workforce. You may recall the previous references to the prison population being mainly male, whereas we see that forensic psychologists seem to be around just 17% male.

Of course, the forensic psychologists registered on the HCPC website are not all working in prisons; however, if this ratio is fairly consistent, we see a workforce which does not reflect the client group in gender terms. This is before we start considering other factors such as ethnicity.

As psychologists, we need to be mindful of the impact we may have. In gender terms, the forensic psychology workforce as a whole is not representative of the population we work with. This seems to be a much more fundamental issue for forensic psychologists than for other domains where, whilst women may dominate the profession, the client group will largely be less male dominated. There may not be a great deal we as individuals can do about that, apart from ensuring that our practice accounts for the potential barriers it may cause and in senior positions seek to reduce imbalance as much as possible. But if you are thinking about the next stage of training – supervised professional practice – it is worth thinking about these imbalances and barriers, how they might affect your practice and how you might navigate the challenge. Certainly, the male prisons are a very male environment – whilst we have seen increases in the number of women prison officers and governors and probation staffs are often women, the environment remains male dominated. At the interview, showing some understanding and strategy of what this may mean for you and how you may approach

Table 2.2 Forensic psychologists, HCPC-registered psychologists and prison population by ethnicity

	Forensic psychologists	All HCPC-registered psychologists	Prison population
Not recorded	0	0	900
Recorded	1,745	26,940	86,052
White	1,515 (87%)	22,605 (84%)	62,403 (73%)
Asian	65 (4%)	1,395 (5%)	7,120 (8%)
Black	35 (2%)	510 (2%)	10,398 (12%)
Mixed	50 (3%)	830 (3%)	4,104 (5%)
Other	20 (1%)	515 (2%)	2,027 (2%)
Prefer not to say	60 (3%)	1,085 (4%)	Incl in not recorded
Total	1,745	26,940	86,952

Source: HCPC Diversity report (2023) www.hcpc-uk.org/resources/data/2023/diversity-data-practitioner-psychologists-2023/

some of these challenges will present you more favourably than somebody who has not considered their own personal impact at all. That is not to say that male forensic psychologists will find this work a breeze – there are different challenges ahead.

We mentioned ethnicity, so Table 2.2 gives a quick breakdown of the registered psychologist workforce as well as the forensic psychologists by ethnicity compared to the prison population from the July 2023 data. We see real differences in the recorded ethnicity of forensic psychologists compared to the wider psychological profession and to those we work with in prisons. Whilst many efforts are underway to balance some of these differences in protected characteristics, there is a long way to go.

Personal Qualities

To become a qualified and effective forensic psychologist, the National Careers Service website suggests you should have:

- Knowledge of psychology
- Counselling skills including active listening and a non-judgemental approach

- Analytical thinking skills
- The ability to understand people's reactions
- Sensitivity and understanding
- The ability to accept criticism and work well under pressure
- Patience and the ability to remain calm in stressful situations
- Excellent written communication skills
- To be able to use a computer and the main software packages competently

(National Careers Service, 2020, https://
nationalcareers.service.gov.uk/job-profiles/
forensic-psychologist)

We think this is a real shame and very much prefer aspects from the previous 2015 list to the 2020 version and would add back in: a genuine desire to help offenders, resilience and the ability to organise a complex workload, as well as patience, empathy, honesty and integrity.

Indeed, a good supervisor would be looking to identify and develop all of the above skills and attitudes in a trainee, as these remain central principles in becoming a good forensic psychologist in our view.

You will also need a range of personal qualities in this field. It goes without saying that you will be bright and academically able in order to gain your degree and access the training route you choose.

However, outside of the theory and knowledge framework of understanding, we would argue a good forensic psychologist must demonstrate three key skills – communication, resilience and an ability to apply evidence-based defensible decision-making.

We asked a range of forensic psychology managers and supervisors what they look for in new trainees. The following quote neatly summarises the answers we received.

Some things can be taught during your training; others are qualities, which we would say you really need to succeed or to get onto a training course. So, if you don't have all of these traits, don't worry too much – but you need to know that it's something that you have the capacity to achieve.

It is easy to assume you have the first two – communication skills and resilience – but an often overlooked element of communication is *listening*. Of course, it may sound obvious to some, but being able to listen to others, reflect on what you have heard and then communicate

> *'Key skills I look for are problem solving, resilience, ability to multi-task, good communication skills – (as well as verbal skills – ability to write well – good grammar, able to proof read, able to adapt to audience) ability to take feedback. Key attitudes – able to adapt to change, belief in rehabilitation. An ability to see the bigger picture is highly desirable – understanding where psychology fits into the wider world of criminal justice. An ability to relate to others and perspective take is very important – both for working with prisoners and prison staff.'*

appropriately in response is a fundamental aspect of being a good practitioner psychologist.

Good communication skills also mean being able to juggle a range of complex and often conflicting pieces of information simultaneously, synthesise these strands into a coherent, balanced and informed position and to explain your professional opinion in clear, easy-to-understand language. This may be in writing, whilst on your feet with staff or offenders or in more formal evidence-giving situations under the pressure of cross-examination. Academic prowess alone does not provide this flexibility and responsivity, and often the pace of delivery is required. Related is the general need for excellent communication and listening skills to help you work with a broad range of people, including other professionals, some of whom may be like you, but many of whom will come from very different walks of life with a range of different experiences. Whilst this skill can be taught to some extent, your innate ability to do this is important. So, the question is, are you able to write well? Can you hold several potentially conflicting positions in your head and synthesise an argument? Can you listen, understand, think on your feet and communicate back?

Another personal quality is a desire to help people. We might say that we would expect this from most, if not all, practitioner psychologists. For forensic psychologists, we would expect you to want to help and support offenders. Whilst protecting the public is a core aim of forensic psychology, the desire to help and not judge others is a core requirement of any role. The setting in which you apply your skills may vary, and you may feel more comfortable within some settings than others due to the 'purpose' of the setting (e.g. health vs. prisons). Your preference for a work setting will vary depending on your particular attributes and interests as well as values and beliefs.

The other quality we mentioned in this section was resilience. There is significant literature about resilience, what it is, how one gets it and how one maintains it. We suggest you read some of this and reflect on whether you are that type of person. If in doubt, talk to some trusted others about this. We also must recognise that an individual's resilience can wane for reasons outside of the workplace. No one is perfect, but moving into a career which can have some impact on your well-being if you are not generally a resilient type would seem foolish. Some would characterise 'resilience' as 'bounce-back-ability', and this is an important part of it. However, the ability to bounce back from challenging or difficult experiences is one part of resilience; another would be the ability to remain objective and non-judgemental in the face of challenging situations. This does not mean you have to be some kind of android – devoid of emotion and exercising algorithmic decision-making – you are your own person, with your own set of experiences, and you will bring your humanity to the role.

It is important to be realistic and to reflect on your own life experiences and how these have contributed to your own personality development and response to particular situations. You should remember that often your day will be filled with exposure to very challenging or difficult information about someone's life history, their actions and behaviour and the consequences of these actions, and you might also be faced with negative or hostile individuals. Objectivity is essential, but it is important that you do not turn into an android and are able to inflect your professional objectivity with normal human traits including empathy and an awareness of 'victimology'. You should carefully think about your own life history and whether you have the capacity to deal with such difficult information at times which may have an emotional impact on you – and indeed how you will manage any such situations, your own coping and support systems and consider your ability to recover from a possible dent to your own resilience.

We don't want to put you off, and of course resilience can be developed and maintained, but we really would suggest that an inner strength or confidence is needed here. Of course, working in prisons is different from working in health settings or in academia – each brings its own set of challenges. As authors, we have very different forensic backgrounds, and we know what our strengths and weaknesses are. So, some of this is about good insight and understanding, which will come with time. Forensic psychology is also a big enough field that a role can be found, or indeed, some may choose to develop into a different domain of psychology.

Now that we've said all that you might be wondering why anyone would want to become a forensic psychologist, as it can be lonely and frequently disturbing work and we're painting a picture of a challenging environment and the need for fast communication and high resilience! Not exactly a sales job! But if you are still with us and think this still sounds like something you might be interested in, then hopefully you're the right fit!

We know why we came into it, but it's a few years ago now, so we asked a number of more recent entrants to the profession:

> *If I'm honest, I can't really remember . . . during my under-graduate degree I wasn't sure what I wanted to do, like many undergraduates I thought I might be interested in clinical psychology, but I wasn't really sure what that was if I'm hon-est. I gained an opportunity to work with a family friend at a prison. I attended weekly with the visiting Community Psychiatric Team and spent time observing assessments of both male and female prisoners. It was so interesting, perhaps in a voyeuristic way. The offences committed and the life experiences of the people were so extreme. I did this for one year before I gradu-ated. [Sophie, (recently achieved Chartered Status, Registered Forensic Psychologist)]*

We find a lot of forensic psychologists became interested in forensics as an 'alternative' to clinical due to the competition to enter clinical training. But over time, the competition to gain a forensic trainee role has also stiffened, along with increased awareness of forensic psychology as a profession, so we see fewer of these.

> *I studied Law as an undergraduate degree after my A Levels and found myself spending more time in the forensic section of the Library rather than working on the legal cases given as assignments. I realised I was more interested in the motivations and background circumstances of why crimes were committed rather than dealing with the consequences (court, convictions, etc.). I therefore felt that Forensic Psychology would be the pathway to take. [Theon, Chartered Psychologist and Registered Forensic Psychologist]*

We also see a fair few non-psychology undergraduates take conversion courses to achieve their Graduate Basis for Chartership (GBC) with the BPS and then enter the forensic field. It's possible, and an understanding of law or wider criminal justice contexts is really important whether studied formally or gained via more informal means.

So, we would say there is no doubt that working in the forensic field can be a very rewarding career, and the challenge of this type of work appeals to many. But it can take an emotional toll on your and also your family. It's important to be aware of this, to recognise the sorts of things you may find more difficult and thus ensure there is some kind of support available for you, both formal and informal. The resilience literature referred to provides some ideas about this.

The final point we mentioned is the ability to utilise an evidence base for defensible decisions. The content here can be trained, as well as some of the skills, but there is an underlying ability to draw on evidence, not act from the gut.

Becoming a Forensic Psychologist

What is the route towards becoming a registered forensic psychologist? Here is a quick overview of the conventional steps, which will be discussed in significantly more detail in Chapter 4.

You will need:

1. A BPS-accredited degree in psychology, leading to GBC, or have undertaken a degree in another subject and undertaken a conversion course (see Chapter 1 for further details). To enrol in a BPS-accredited degree, you will usually need five GCSEs (C/4 or above), plus three A-levels, but do check with course providers for their exact entry requirements. A list of all BPS-accredited courses can be found on the BPS website www.bps.org.uk/.

   It is usually a good idea to take a final-year option in forensic psychology, if this is available to you, or to base your dissertation in this area if possible. There are also now more undergraduate forensic psychology degree courses available. However, these are not a requirement for entry to a forensic psychology MSc and some regard them as specialising too early. Check that a forensic undergraduate degree won't make your career options more limited if you choose not to follow a forensic path – do clinical and counselling training look favourably upon them? Or do they prefer a more general psychology undergraduate training?

   If you are doing a combined honours, that is, psychology combined with another subject, please check with your course provider that any option choices you make in your course do not take you away from GBC accreditation – we have known a number of psychology and criminology graduates take a little too much criminology and not enough psychology and graduate with an excellent degree, but without sufficient credits in the psychology side to achieve GBC. Please check and keep checking as you progress through your degree!

2. An HCPC-approved programme of postgraduate training leading to registration as a forensic psychologist.

   Once you have GBC, you will need to continue your training and work towards registration with the HCPC and, in most cases, Chartered membership of the BPS. You can do this by completing the following and then applying to register with the HCPC ww.hcpc.org.uk

i)   A BPS-accredited master's degree in forensic psychology
     In order to access the next stage of becoming a forensic psychologist, you will need a BPS-accredited master's degree (MSc) in forensic psychology. You can access the full list of approved courses via the BPS website, and this list is ever-growing; new courses may take on students prior to achieving BPS accreditation – please check the status of courses to ensure they will meet the standards required. Each of these courses will have its own identity and entry criteria and some might be integrated with further postgraduate study – such as a professional doctorate or HCPC-approved route to registration (see below and later for details). But achieving a good master's level QFP will certainly give you options for the next stage, and this is discussed further in Chapter 4.

ii) Supervised practice in forensic settings
     Often referred to as 'Stage 2' or 'Stage 2 equivalent', this is your 'on the job' learning, which can be achieved in a variety of ways.

In your early years as a trainee forensic psychologist, you will generally be either working for an organisation whilst training or self-funding an HCPC-taught course which you complete full-time whilst undertaking practice placements, which provide you with a breadth of experience.

If employed as a trainee, you can expect a salary in the region of £30K–36K (at the time of writing). This is likely to increase to around £50K+ once registered depending on the role, setting, etc. This salary will then continue to increase over time; at present, the demand for forensic psychologists (registered, not trainees) outstrips supply, hence the growth in private practice!

There are a number of different training routes available to qualify as a forensic psychologist, and these are evolving and developing all the time. Although it can seem to be confusing, see Chapter 4 for a fuller description of what is available at the time of writing, but here is a flow chart to try to help you map out the routes available!

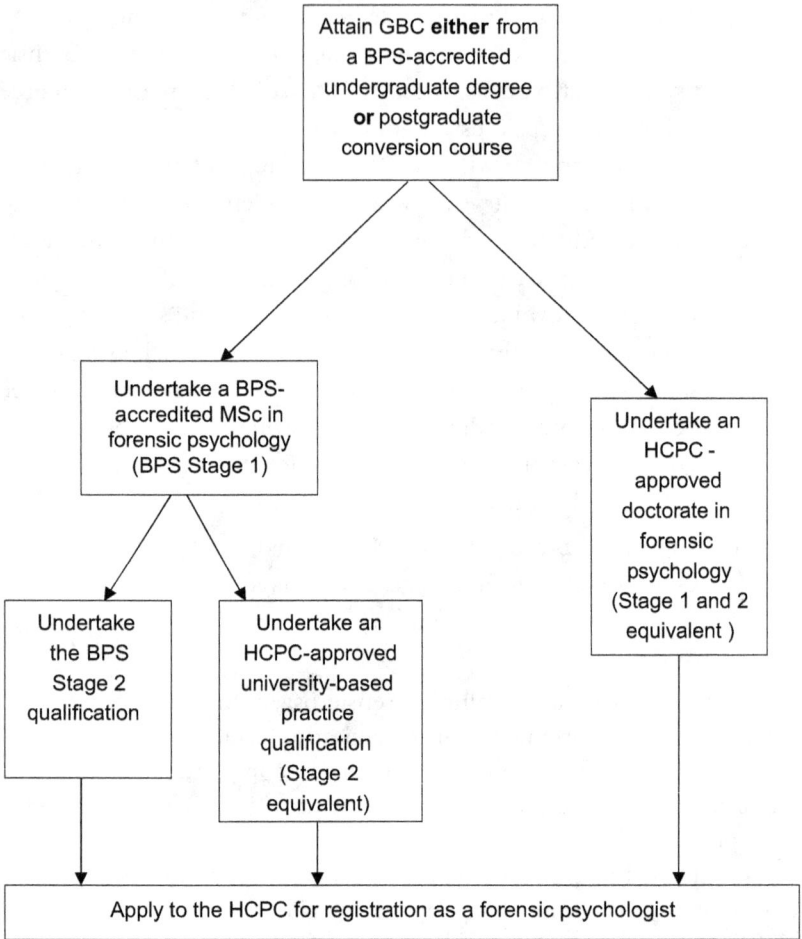

Figure 2.1 Flow chart of routes to becoming a registered forensic psychologist.

3 | Psychology Graduates – The Next Steps

- Outline of Master's courses
- Outline of Stage 1 of the forensic qualification
- How should students approach their master's?
- What will they learn?
- What can they do outside the course to help their career?

Beginning the Journey

Two of the most popular final-year options for students taking a psychology degree accredited by the BPS are modules related to clinical psychology and forensic psychology. This is often because of the career opportunities these options may offer but is also because many psychology undergraduates find these specialist areas both interesting and challenging. Moreover, they provide evidence for how psychology can be usefully applied not only to study criminal behaviour but also to explore what motivates offenders in order to help them make positive changes in their lives. As stated earlier, communication and listening skills are essential in order to work effectively with a broad range of people, including other professionals.

We asked academic colleagues how their interest in forensic psychology had begun, and these were some of their responses:

DOI: 10.4324/9781315675831-3

> *My interest in understanding 'crime' began with the 'discovery'*
> *of widespread child sexual abuse in the 1980s and associated*
> *media coverage and the launch of Childline; and later youth*
> *work with vulnerable children and those who had come to the*
> *attention of police/probation/social services.*

> *Through reading books such as 'The Jigsaw Man' by Paul Britton*

> *I did not begin my career in forensic psychology with an inter-*
> *est specifically in crime, although like many others I was always*
> *somewhat seduced by the sexiness of television programmes to do*
> *with crime or criminal behaviour. That said, 'Cracker' was the*
> *big one in my day and there wasn't really anything particularly*
> *'sexy' about that programme! But over the years I discovered that*
> *although I had first been interested in clinical psychology as a*
> *career, I was in fact more interested in the extremes of human*
> *behaviour. Why did people do things that many other people were*
> *apparently incapable of doing and what contributed to this sort*
> *of decision making, justification of their actions and a failure to*
> *understand the consequence of their actions on others, particularly*
> *victims of their crimes? Was there anything we could do to help*
> *treat/prevent such things happening? And was anyone trying to*
> *help those who needed help to change their behaviour? It was then*
> *that I discovered there was a potential career open to me which*
> *would allow me to develop this interest and work with a group*
> *of people who hopefully I might not otherwise meet in my day-to-*
> *day life. Forensic Psychology seemed like a perfect fit incorporating*
> *a clinical approach balanced with a theoretical understanding*
> *of a confluence of variables – personality, individual experience,*
> *welfare/social psychology, impact of social policy and environmen-*
> *tal/contextual influences to behaviour. I am pleased to say that*
> *this initial interest developed into a rewarding and in my view,*
> *important career pathway and one I have never regretted taking.*

> *I had thought I might do occupational psychology, but my crimi-nology 3rd-year module really grabbed my attention. After a couple of years working in an unrelated field I decided to take the plunge and do a Criminology Masters and then moved into forensic psychology. I've never regretted it. For me it's about enabling change – whether that be working with an individual or developing new regimes or policies or practices – as a forensic psychologist you can make a real difference to a lot of lives.*

So, if forensic psychology is still your career choice after reading this far, you should aim to achieve an upper second in your undergraduate degree, and ideally, your final-year dissertation topic[i] would be related to forensic issues so that you can showcase your interest in this area as well as your academic skills.

HCPC and BPS Differences

The Distinct Roles of the HCPC and the BPS in Relation to Training

As mentioned earlier, the HCPC is the statutory regulator for practi-tioner psychologists in the United Kingdom; it also regulates several other health professions including physiotherapy, occupational ther-apy and paramedics. In relation to training, the role of the HCPC is to approve training programmes that are designed to develop all of the competencies required to practise in a particular health profes-sion. This means that someone who has successfully completed the programme can apply to be automatically registered with HCPC. In the case of forensic psychology, the BPS Stage 2 qualification, uni-versity-based doctorates (which incorporate Stage 1 and Stage 2) and university-based Stage 2 equivalent qualifications are all approved by the HCPC.

Stage 1 MSc courses do not lead directly to eligibility for registra-tion, and therefore, the HCPC does not approve these courses. Instead, the BPS operates an accreditation system for Stage 1 MSc forensic psychology programmes (in the same way as it does for undergraduate programmes).

All forensic psychologists (and other practitioner psychologists) must maintain registration with the HCPC in order to practise. Once qualified, forensic psychologists are eligible to become Chartered Psychologists with the BPS and then become full members of the Division of Forensic Psychology. There are lots of benefits to belonging to the BPS, but membership is not required to practise.

Someone who has not completed an HCPC-approved qualification cannot use the relevant protected title, although they may be a Chartered member of the BPS.

Postgraduate Qualification

The next step for you is to consider applying to enrol in an accredited master's course in forensic psychology or a forensic psychology-related doctorate. As stated previously, a list of accredited courses can be found on the BPS website (bps.org.uk).

BPS-accredited master's courses in forensic psychology generally follow a standard route and may be either one year full-time or two years part-time. Some of these courses may be available for online or part-time study. Thus, they provide you with a variety of options in terms of cost and flexibility to complete them. These courses provide an approved curriculum with standard lectures and seminars, together with tutorial support and dissertation supervision. As with achieving GBC, be sure that your MSc is BPS accredited and will provide your first step towards forensic training. New courses need to run prior to receiving their accreditation, which of course is not always a sure thing. You are looking to see that your MSc provides eligibility to access Stage 2 of forensic training.

Professional doctorate programmes are an alternative (integrated) way of achieving your MSc – sometimes you will need to complete the MSc component of the course prior to 'converting' to the doctoral programme, and different eligibility might also be in place. But courses offer different routes, so do your research!

For a Forensic MSc to be accredited by the BPS, they need to cover key components. Whilst the university it sits in and the research interests of the course leaders may impact aspects of the programme content, core components include:

- Critically evaluating the current knowledge, theory and evidence base relevant to the discipline (note: this may comprise both psychological theory and knowledge from other disciplines) and understanding that this is an important first step for all work and activities;
- Identifying and developing skills and capabilities relevant to the progression of forensic psychology practice;
- Using a range of techniques and research methods applicable to psychological enquiry;
- Applying relevant ethical, legal and professional practice frameworks (e.g. BPS and HCPC) and maintaining appropriate professional boundaries;
- Communicating effectively (verbally and nonverbally) with colleagues, research supervisors and a wider audience;
- Critically reflecting on and synthesising all of the above to inform their developing professional identity as a Forensic Psychologist in Training; and
- Communicating their work appropriately in a range of appropriate written (e.g. professional reports (including those written in formats suitable for journal papers, conference posters [or similar], and oral formats (e.g. presentations, one-to-one feedback etc).

(*British Psychological Society*, 2024)

At the master's level, you will be expected to undertake a significant degree of independent study, especially in relation to your dissertation, and whilst tutorial support will be provided, the focus at this level of study is independent research, so excellent library skills are essential, and tutorials on these will be offered in most university libraries. Developing a critical faculty in relation to reviewing research papers and producing original commentary on them is a vital component of the master's study, and you will be able to demonstrate your acquisition of these skills in your dissertation. In any event, a good MSc course should give you a clear grounding in theories applying to the discipline and you should have contact with a range of professionals who have both research and practical experience in forensic psychology. You will no doubt judge the suitability of a course on a variety of factors including geography, reputation, areas of specialism and others, but the main criteria you should consider is whether the course is accredited by the BPS. Employers should not demonstrate any particular bias to any particular programme (unless there is a clear contractual basis or relationship in place), but the standard of BPS accreditation is essential for progression into Stage 2 or beginning the training component of your qualification as a forensic psychologist. In short, if you want to become a forensic psychologist, you need to complete a master's programme which is accredited by the BPS – which one you choose tends to matter less than the accreditation being achieved.

Postgraduate forensic courses change, gain and lose accreditation, so it's best to check the BPS website to see what the current offer is rather than us providing you with a list here. Check the accredited courses list on the BPS website under 'careers and education' and apply the search criteria you need (https://portal.bps.org.uk/Accredited-Courses).

When we spoke to students undertaking master's courses in forensic psychology, they indicated that they had found their courses stimulating for a range of reasons, some of which are outlined below:

> *I felt that the more applied parts/modules of the Masters were very stimulating because they provided the opportunity to make the link between research and real-life practice.*

> *I really enjoyed my course though it was hard work, and I particularly liked the modules which were related to practice. However, there were some aspects of the course which I did not find beneficial, such as the module on Law. . . . Additionally, I think that some of the assignments were quite difficult for students not yet working in a forensic environment.*

Some students felt that their courses could have offered more within the curriculum, for example:

> *I felt that more coverage could have been provided in relation to reflective practice, especially as this is a large part of Stage 2 (BPS). More content in relation to the practical skills needed in the field, such as interview techniques, would also have been useful, as would more content in relation to Personality Disorders and Psychopathy within the prison population.*

On completion of your master's course, we would expect you to be able to demonstrate:

- The ability to use a range of relevant techniques and research methods, including both quantitative and qualitative methodologies
- A critical understanding of the psychological theories and evidence of relevance to processes in the justice system, including the legal framework of the civil and criminal justice system, processes of investigation, the process of detention and interdisciplinary working
- A critical understanding of different approaches to assessment and formulation in assessing individuals, groups and organisations

Successful completion of a master's course should therefore fulfil the initial requirements of training in forensic psychology. This knowledge and understanding, and the associated core skills, will support you in your progression to the next stage, where you can begin to develop your practice under supervision. More about this in Chapter 4.

Work Experience

Whilst studying at the master's level, it is extremely helpful if you can find forensic-related work experience, either voluntary or paid. This will boost your curriculum vitae (CV) whilst also providing an opportunity to assess whether this career route is for you. If you are thinking about embarking on a professional doctorate, HCPC registration route or indeed the BPS Stage 2 route to qualification, then having some relevant work experience is likely a prerequisite (more about these later).

There are a variety of things you can do. For example, taking on a role such as supporting the Listener Scheme, which aims to reduce suicide and self-harm in prisons, can provide such an opportunity. Volunteers with the Samaritans organisation are trained to support prisoners to become listeners in relation to their fellow prisoners. They provide confidential emotional support to those who may be struggling to cope with imprisonment. The first Listener Scheme was introduced at HMP Swansea in 1991, and now, almost all prisons in England, Scotland and Wales operate these schemes. At the last count, there were more than 1,500 listeners in UK prisons and over 74,000 requests for support from prisoners. It is worth checking with potential supervisors or course leaders whether the work experience you are considering meets the requirements for the next stage.

In the community, you may want to explore possibilities of working as a volunteer befriender, shadowing mental health or psychological services or exploring the third sector – there are often volunteering opportunities available with mental health or homelessness charities, for example. An organisation such as Circles UK seeks to build safer communities through local volunteers working with sex offenders to minimise alienation, support reintegration and so prevent sexual reoffending. Their website states,

> A 'Circle of Support and Accountability' is a group of Volunteers from a local community which forms a 'circle' around an offender. In Circles, the sex offender is referred to as the 'Core Member'. Each Circle consists of four to six Volunteers and a Core Member. It aims to provide a supportive social network that also requires the Core Member to take responsibility (be 'accountable') for his/her ongoing risk management. The Circle can also provide support and practical guidance in such things as developing their social skills, finding suitable accommodation or helping the Core Member to find appropriate hobbies and interests.

Gaining any similar work experience would prove invaluable, and being in a position to discuss the benefits of your work experience in the field of forensic psychology would be a significant advantage at the interview.

4 | Becoming a Trainee

- Applying for a trainee position
- What they're looking for at the interview
- Life as a trainee
- Making the most of placements
- Working with a mentor
- Lots of testimonials

It is helpful to know yourself quite well. How resilient are you? Are you a team player? What are your own personal strengths and weaknesses, and how might they affect this career? Which environment might best suit you if you do pursue a forensic psychology career, and why?

As we've said, forensic psychology is a challenging but exciting field to be in. It is as equally rewarding and fascinating as it is draining and difficult.

We have signposted a range of options, choices and thoughts you need to consider, and you are now at the stage where you've made the decision to continue and you need to get trained. Of course, nothing is simple in forensic psychology, and your pathway might be:

i) Employed as a trainee undertaking training via whichever route
ii) Self-funded on a university course, completing placements organised by the university
iii) Employed not as a trainee, but in a CJS undertaking training via whichever route
iv) Employed not as a trainee, not in a CJS undertaking training via whichever route

DOI: 10.4324/9781315675831-4

Each of these pathways offers its own issues, costs and timescale – the more independent route (or 'BPS route', as it is sometimes called) requires you to be organised, source your own supervisor and be mature and responsible for your own learning and development (although if you're employed in a trainee position, much of this is likely done by your employer). The BPS offers specialised registrars to support you in the qualification and has mandatory courses for supervisors to attend. This means that you should know or be able to find out whether your supervisor is properly trained and aware of the requirements of Chartership, and through meeting them and having discussions, you can establish whether you can work with them. It also means that although the route is more independent and offered usually at a far cheaper cost than alternative routes, you still have the BPS supporting you and you can speak to your registrars for any additional support or guidance you might need. It is possible that as a trainee, you might experience a power difference between yourself and the supervisor and not know how to resolve difficulties or issues. The independent route does not leave you out there, on your own, removing your paddle and sending you up the creek! On this route, you will still have the support of experienced staff and an experienced board, who can help you with any questions or issues that might arise. With the 'new qualification' (still new at the time of writing and launched in 2021), the submission requirements are clear, well-structured and offer several points for formative feedback before the final submission goes in. Details are available on the DFP website, and the BPS continues to consider this route as the 'gold standard'. Check out the forensic qualification through the BPS website careers and education/BPS qualifications for the most up-to-date position.

You may pick up chatter about the independent route taking people years to complete. Indeed, this used to be true, with some trainees spending many, many years completing this route. But that is no longer the case. The 'new' qualification has made significant strides to avoid that, and you will now know exactly how long it will take you to be qualified once you have done your master's. This will be two, three or four years depending on your experience, and you even have the option of shifting between the 'tracks'. The route is designed to be flexible with a known end-point, so nobody is left wondering when they might be qualified. It offers flexibility and retains the assurance of quality, which has made this route so popular over the years. The following is an edited extract from the qualification handbook provided to candidates once they are registered on this 'independent' BPS route:

> *You can choose to enrol on a 2, 3 or 4-year track depending on whether you work on a full-time or part-time basis and your access to relevant development opportunities. It is important to note that this relates to the assessment points for your written submissions, and not the time-frame for completion of the qualification. The assessment schedule is designed so that you submit work at set points according to whether you are enrolled on a 2, 3 or 4-year track. Following your final submission, you will also need to satisfy the assessors at a viva, and you will need to bear this in mind when considering the overall timeframe for completion.*
>
> *You must be either employed on a full or part-time basis in order to undertake the QFP (Stage 2) and must be working a minimum of 0.5 WTE. However, this figure will only allow you to achieve the minimum number of days of enrolment (460 days) and as such, candidates are encouraged to work for a minimum of 0.6 WTE or more in order to give them some degree of flexibility.*
>
> *You can request to move from one enrolment track to another, subject to receipt of a suitable plan of training update and the Registrar's approval. In some circumstances, it is possible that the Qualifications Board will recommend that you switch to a different enrolment track based on the level of progression and/or competence evidenced in your submissions, or if your submission deadlines are extended for any reason. It is important to note that candidates cannot progress until all elements of the formative assessment are complete.*

Whilst some of the challenges of the 'independent route' might include finding a suitable placement(s) to offer the breadth of experience you need as well as the opportunities for research, many of the trainees on this route prefer the flexibility it offers, the independent nature of learning and the cheaper cost and will benefit from the new structure and time limits on qualification in the version which was launched in 2021. This means you do not get 'stuck' in a particular trainee role and are supported to move through the qualification process.

If you are employed as a trainee, your employer should be considering your placements, your development and wider support to progress you. This will provide you with structure, so it's not entirely 'independent', but there can be conflicting demands between your training needs and organisational delivery at times.

Some trainees, however, prefer an even more structured route, which can support them in finding suitable placements if they are not employed, as they might have existing relationships with placement providers and a carefully structured system of support provided by a university. These courses tend to be professional doctorate routes provided by universities (an updated list can be found via the HCPC website) and, in addition to the Chartership level of qualification, offer the additional bonus of being called 'Dr'! For some, having that title is important and they feel it adds to their credibility. The BPS route does not yet offer the use of the title, although it is pitched at the doctoral level, and indeed, all professional doctorate courses are accredited by the BPS to meet the requirements of the qualification anyway. The university doctoral routes tend to be more expensive but can be a bit shorter if you are able to keep to the deadlines, although, with the new BPS route, there is not much difference in the time it might take to be qualified. The main difference would be the use of the title 'Dr'. An increasing number of these courses are popping up, so it is worth exploring this option when you are ready and always useful to talk to qualified psychologists and see what their experience has been of different routes. You should note that often (but not always) the placements offered by universities tend to be unpaid, whereas the independent route does usually offer the opportunity for paid roles to form part of your experience. This is not a hard-and-fast rule though, so you should do a little digging when you are exploring these options and see which one works best for you.

One thing you do need to be aware of is neither route is 'easy', and whilst some may find some bits of some routes 'easier' than others, you should not underestimate that the process of training and meeting the requirements for submission – whichever route you take – is going to dominate your life for the time you are on it. And in a way, that's OK – you are going to be dealing with some very bad people who have done some very bad things, some very troubled people who have done some very troubling things and some very complex people who have done what they have done for very complex reasons. Your job is not only to help them but also to help the public – both in terms of protection and in contributing to the narrative of understanding people's actions at a profoundly human level. So, it is a very responsible thing to do, and it should take lots of your attention and energy to try and get it right. But don't forget that you still have to have a life or you'll be no good to anyone, and finding the right balance between the effort you need to put into qualifying and the life you need to live to make it all means something is a tricky thing to do and requires some mature decision-making. This might even inform which route you choose to take. We explore some of the issues facing trainees in choosing a setting for their work in more detail below.

Working as a Trainee Forensic Psychologist

Once you have considered what setting your own skills and interests may best suit, the first thing you will need to think about is what experience and academic qualifications an applicant for a particular trainee position may need. Whilst the previous chapter talked about the next steps and MSc courses along with a little about the doctorate forensic training courses, it is still the case that some posts advertised as trainee forensic psychologists do not require an MSc in advance of appointment.

So, by the time you are considering applying for a trainee post, you may or may not have applied for or completed your MSc in forensic psychology, and the trainee positions available will vary as to whether they require completion of the MSc or whether they will only require GBC with the BPS.

So:

- For some trainee positions, you will need your GBC but will complete the MSc and train towards qualified status whilst in the trainee post. The MSc costs and time away from work may or may not be funded by the organisation.
- For others, you will be expected to have already achieved your MSc to be eligible for a trainee post and would then complete your supervised practice training to qualified status.

Some employers have non-trainee posts, where you may be able to complete your MSc (sometimes with financial support) with opportunities to then move into a trainee post. For example, HMPPS requires an MSc for a trainee forensic psychologist post but does have some methods of offering financial assistance and study time away from work to a cohort of 'Interventions Facilitators/Groupworkers', who are then ideally placed to apply for promotion when trainee posts are internally advertised. They are also currently reviewing the introduction of an assistant forensic psychologist as well as offering sandwich course placements. Similarly, sometimes, the police and some hospital settings provide either financial support or study time for those in non-trainee roles to complete academic courses. It is always worth looking at innovative ideas in a range of criminal justice settings.[i]

The eligibility requirements for trainee posts can also change over time, so it is important that you review the position when making decisions about whether to self-fund to complete an MSc, find an employer who will support this when you are in a trainee post or work for an employer before applying for trainee posts.

MSc courses and trainee posts both ask for a level of 'experience'. For some people, this can be a 'Catch-22' situation, that is, you can't get on an MSc because you have no experience, but some organisations won't give you any experience until you are on an MSc course. For that reason, you need to think laterally about the types of experience you can get and how you can best map your experience to the posts you are applying for. The previous chapter touched on some work experience options.

There are obviously a range of options for gaining experience, for example, asking for placements within the types of organisations that offer trainee posts. Some opportunities do exist, but they are usually few and the demand is high.

Sometimes, experience within the criminal justice system can be found without being directly involved in psychology. This may be helpful, but what will really matter is how you apply your experience and learning to the posts you are after – understanding and articulating your transferable skills is the key.

We spoke to a range of forensic psychologists, both in training roles and registered, to see how they had approached this issue:

I found it tough to get a trainee position. I worked at a Magistrates' Court before joining the Prison Service which I think was invaluable in gaining experience within the criminal justice field. Any related experience will really help your chances of success. I then worked 8.5 years in a psychological assistant post before securing a full-time Trainee post. You need perseverance and tenacity if you want to follow this route. Be sure it is what you want and if it is go for it! Don't give up!

I worked voluntarily at a Therapeutic Community to get started on the training route at the same time as continuing with my role at the time as Psychological Assistant (condensed my working hours into 4 days) in order to do so. I think this prepared me well for my eventual successful interview as I had some experience of what the role involved. I attended many interviews before being successful. At the time I thought I was ready but on reflection I wasn't quite there. I think timing is everything! Also no trainee post is the same, which is worth thinking about. Do you want to be a Treatment Manager? Do you want to work with young people or sex offenders? There are lots of different roles under the umbrella of trainee.

I would suggest that those wanting to be a trainee ensure that they gain experience of working in a forensic setting first, either as a volunteer or in a paid role. This can include, for example, working as a facilitator on offender behaviour programmes, as a healthcare assistant in a forensic mental health unit, or as a mentor/support worker in a Youth Offending Service. This will help to increase confidence in interacting professionally with offenders and/or victims and the range of staff who are involved in their supervision and management. Such experiences provide the opportunity for developing team working skills and motivating people to change, as well as seeing risk assessment, treatment and management processes in action. They further test out individuals' comfort in working within forensic environments, including those with stringent security procedures (locked gated, bars, CCTV, etc.), something that can feel oppressive for many people. It will also help to develop and strengthen the resilience that is crucial to working in our challenging profession. Opportunities for working closely with experienced forensic psychologists are also valuable as those interested in pursuing this type of career will see first-hand what is involved in the role. They should learn very quickly that the work of a forensic psychologist bears little resemblance to those portrayed in the media.

We've indicated that working in a forensic setting isn't for everyone, and for some, they will be best suited to particular types of forensic settings. Prior to making too much of a financial and emotional commitment, it is best to understand if this world will suit you and, if it will, which type of setting. Some forensic psychologists can effectively and happily function across settings; others find particular organisations that best meet their own styles and values. Some find, sometimes too late after time, money and emotional investment have been spent, that a forensic role is not for them. This is fine. It's not failure, and realising this will be best both for your own future and for those of service users with whom you may have worked. It may be that a different domain of psychology is a better fit or an alternative career altogether. This is well said in the following quote from a senior forensic psychologist manager and supervisor:

I think it is important for people to realise that working in a forensic setting isn't for everyone so it's helpful if people have a sense of what their reaction to working in such an environment is likely to be. Self-awareness is crucial.

Training whilst employed in one organisation provides you with experience of that organisation. Other training routes that rotate placements across organisations can provide you with a greater breadth of organisational experiences. There are pros and cons of each, and of course, the pathway you take will very much depend on the opportunities available at that time. Awareness of the gaps in your development (i.e. breadth but less depth or vice versa) is essential, but to be qualified, you must be able to demonstrate a range and breadth of experience with reference to the setting, presenting issues and demographics of your clients.

We start here with the 'employment whilst training' model and will move onto the other options in this section, such as full-time/self-funded doctoral students. It can seem quite confusing at first, so hang in there!

Employed as a Trainee: The Application Process for a Trainee Role

Different organisations have different requirements and different types of application processes. It may sound obvious, but it is important to tailor the application to the needs of the organisation – whether they simply ask for a CV to be submitted or whether they have a more complicated competence-based application form.

You may, or may not, have much forensic experience. Remember – forensic experience can be gained – often what recruiters are looking for is that you meet the minimum academic requirements and that you have applied your own history to the application form/process appropriately. Forensic experience helps; of course, it does, but simply stating you have worked/shadowed/completed a placement in a forensic setting is not enough. Recruiters are often more interested in the individual who can show their resilience, their problem-solving and their motivation through a range of transferable skills and examples. A few examples are below and are carried on within the later 'at interview' section from those who have completed or who are currently on training routes, including many individuals who sift applicants for trainee jobs. Many of these quotes also include examples of experience gained pre-trainee employment.

> *'After finishing my MSc in Forensic Psychology I got a psychological assistant post. . . . . apart from my MSc, I had little direct experience with forensic populations . . . my teamwork competence example was about playing in my local rugby team!. . . . this wasn't seen as a disadvantage but rather it showed transferable skills. And everyone has to start somewhere!'*

> *'A handy hint is to reflect on every role experienced (from netball captain to Saturday job) and see what you got out of it (and link it to a competence where you can). Even doing a paper round as a teenager tells me something about a candidate. Use a variety of examples in the application – they don't all need to be about work either. Breadth of experience is useful – prisons are by their very nature inward facing environments'*

> *'Third sector, health, community Criminal Justice work, client work in other settings have all been rich sources of experience gathering I have seen when reviewing applications.'*

Bear in mind that if the post requires an MSc as part of the eligibility, simply describing that you have one will not differentiate you from the other applicants. You're unique, special and different – you need to understand why and sell it!

What They Are Looking for at Interview

If you've achieved an interview for a trainee post – well done as the competition will have been fierce to get this far. You might also find that the organisation is using an assessment centre approach – more on this later.

Before you go to the interview, you need to ensure that you do your research. You will obviously have done some of this already in identifying the post and successfully completing an application form, but the following points are for you to consider:

- Firstly, the organisation and how it works, issues that are important in that field (i.e. NHS/HMPPS/Police) at the current time that may impact forensic psychology. What is the political climate? What are the aims of the organisation? How does forensic psychology sit within that context?
- Secondly, the post itself; what is the role? What type of work will you be doing, with what client group and in what setting? Understand the reality of the role.
- Thirdly, in relation to your training, what fees do they pay? What time and support are you given to complete your training? Is there a preferred training provider? What happens if one of the academic courses doesn't accept you? Is there a time limit in which you must complete your training? Will you need to pay fees back if you leave soon after qualifying?
- Fourthly, some wider practicalities; is it in one location? Are you expected to travel much? Does the role suit your domestic needs?
- What is the assessment process? Is it a panel interview? An assessment centre? Do you know who will be on the panel? If a large organisation, does it have a particular approach to interviewing?

One piece of advice is don't focus *too* much on your training needs but do sound informed and interested in the training and support package available. Trainee posts vary in how much they are required to perform a job role versus focus on their training. Whilst organisations will want to train you, you are generally paid to do a job when training in forensic psychology and there will be expectations regarding your delivery of work outputs and objectives, not simply how an organisation will train you. Some posts might be more heavily weighted as 'training' posts that are supernumerary, but these are few and far between; ask about the balance (or tension) between training and delivery and what the organisational expectations are of you to be sure you are clear of both the psychological and actual contracts you are entering into. Potential trainees who understand the training route and view themselves as active participants who can drive their own development stand out from those who don't.

Below, we have a few suggestions from the psychology managers and recruiters we spoke to:

> *In preparing for the interview really get to know the route. Find out what the core roles are, speak to someone already in training and think about the competencies you have that would make you a good psychologist. It takes more than just talking to offenders.*

> *Many organisations which recruit Forensic Psychologists in Training will use a competency-based framework to assess candidates at interview. Quite understandably, candidates are often keen to promote their forensic qualifications on interview. However, what is important to remember is that all the candidates who have made it through to interview will have met the minimum qualification requirements for the organisation, for example an MSc in Forensic Psychology. As such, the interviewers will work on the basis that candidates have demonstrated an academic understanding of the field and will be looking for evidence of the candidates' ability to demonstrate the specific competencies required. Candidates should therefore understand what competencies they are being assessed against and consider experiences they have which help demonstrate those competencies. These experiences can relate to forensic work or be more personal. Some of the most memorable responses to interview questions have been based on situations/experiences that the candidate has faced on a personal level (e.g. Trekking in the Himalaya's) but where they clearly understood how to use that example to demonstrate the competencies interviewers were looking for. So, regardless of whether you have much experience in a forensic setting, make sure you demonstrate the competencies the organisation is looking for!*

The following quote is from a psychologist who themselves went through the recruitment process as a trainee and then – as is often the case – progressed through various stages to become a senior who was responsible for recruitment. It is useful to see their own reflection through personal experience, hindsight and professional recruitment. It contains some useful tips on approaching the whole interview and selection process!

Whilst I can safely say I've never enjoyed any interview experience I did learn the most about my strengths/weaknesses/ the job role from the more intensive interview processes. I also think that because of the nature of the work it is important that applicants' knowledge, skills, strengths and development areas are explored and assessed thoroughly (all said with the benefit of hindsight and having now recovered these experiences!)

Recruiting into trainee positions now, I like to look for an individual that can demonstrate an all-round awareness of the service, its users, and the demands of the role/job. Talking about how you've always been interested in working with notorious serial killers is also a poor selling point when the majority of forensic work is not this! Those who have had some experience of working with offenders, that is, through mentoring or YJB schemes often have a greater understanding which they can demonstrate and use as examples to support their applications/ interviews. However, don't underestimate the value of drawing on your full employment history. I once interviewed a candidate who gave a really good answer to how they would manage working with difficult prisoners by drawing on her experience of working with difficult customers as a waitress during the weekends! It's about the nature of the skills you may already have that you can transfer to a different setting.

From my perspective, there are a number of keys factors that I look for in interviewing trainees. One of the important aspects is to what extent a candidate really understands what being a trainee involves so I find it helpful to ask candidates about what their expectations are of a trainee role, what they are likely to find difficult and how they will overcome barriers – it can be quite clear in interview if a candidate does not have a balanced or informed view of the requirements of a trainee role, which may reflect a lack of planning and preparation for interview. Also, I find it important to gain an idea of their level of knowledge about both the competencies required to become a forensic psychologist and also training routes available, to show they have really considered what training involves, and what is likely to be the best option for them. An understanding of what their own individual developmental needs and priorities are likely to be in the first 12 months of training is also a useful gauge of their understanding of the role.

Excuse the very lengthy testimonial below, but the advice and reflection of this senior psychologist seem useful. No doubt every single potential forensic psychologist will have meticulously scrutinised the wisdom contained in this book, so it is worth looking at the below and thinking about how you can stand out, be professional and become indispensable to a team!

I always feel that on paper the competency scores are often very close, with the best and worst candidates often showing similar profiles. . . . at the end of the day I usually have a strong sense of which candidates excite me and who I would want to be part of my team . . . the basic competencies are what I expect to see . . . however on their own are unlikely to be enough . . . I expect those who turn up to interview to be well presented, well informed, and well prepared . . . to have anticipated my questions . . . not look surprised when I asked them why they want to be a Forensic Psychologist. . . . I expect them to have given this a considerable

> *level of thought. . . . It can sometimes feel that a candidate simply hopes we will like them and give them the job . . . this is a huge investment on both sides. . . . Being a Trainee is far from the finished professional we are looking for. . . . We both need to invest considerable time and effort to get to that point, and I expect them to have thought this through. . . . I want a candidate that not only has met my expectations, in that they can demonstrate (and discuss) the fundamental competencies, but I want someone who has thought through how they will achieve their goals. . . . I want a candidate who I feel I can jointly work with towards a shared goal, that they will invest the same if not more than me in getting there . . . the good candidates should be able to explain the journey they hope to embark on and give examples of similar challenges that they have undertaken and overcome in the past. This is far more important than knowing the legal system or other parts of the role.*

So that is the context for the recruitment process, but it is worth noting that the psychologist recruiter here is already talking about 'investment'. This is an investment in time and money that an individual or organisation is going to make in *you*. They want to know that you are worth it and not just some rote-learnt android that has no aptitude for thinking creatively and making a difference to their peers, their environment and the community, as well as the service users. This particular recruiter feels strongly about this area and goes on to give some useful practical tips on 'standing out'.

> *We can train people with skills and knowledge, but motivation, commitment and determination need to be there from the off. . . . So at the end of a long days interviewing, considering the 6–8 individuals that have attended, who stands out? I imagine they will be the ones who walked in looking prepared and professional. They are probably the ones that have spent time managing their anxieties by practising in front of parents, friends and the mirror. They will look smart but personable and show openness, not fear in response to questioning (I need*

to see this as this shows me they will reflect and respond well to supervision and feedback). I then want to hear how you have researched the route to qualification. I don't want to hear that you want to be a Trainee; I want to hear why you want to be a Qualified Forensic Psychologist. I will be interested to hear how you will work towards this, and although interesting, I am not going to base my decision on the fact you have wanted to be a Forensic Psychologist since you were 12. I may in fact find this a little peculiar. . . . So given that you are prepared, competent, professional and willing to learn, what else is important to me? Alongside all these things, what I really need is someone who can work with others. For this you need to show adaptability and objectivity. This involves balance, careful thought and reflection. I will see this through how you approach the interview and your ability to perform and get your point across under pressure. Being a Forensic Psychologist requires the ability to support others and be supported. Fundamentally I am not looking for a singular trainee; I am looking for someone who can be part of a team. I can accept flaws and weaknesses, believe it or not we are really good at working with the less than perfect, but I am interested in how you respond to these. To be good at the job you will need to be flexible, be able to apply your skills and knowledge as appropriate, and be able to show empathy and objectivity in equal measure. So be prepared, show your determination and don't be afraid to show your personality.

So, how much do you actually need to know about the training itself? We'll let our senior psych answer!

'What I want when recruiting is someone who properly understands the training route – not necessarily all the details – although this is helpful – but what it involves, how it will impact on trainees' lives and a genuine commitment to this. I like to see people who know why they want to be a forensic psychologist – knowing what it means to be Chartered/registered and wants

> to achieve this – rather than just doing this because of a passing interest or because it seems like the next step. I think people undertaking the route need to have given it real thought – (I would imagine people don't sign up for med school on a whim but it sometimes seems that people go through the motions of becoming a trainee just because they see it as the next step without thinking of the end point)'

> 'In terms of experience I think that transferable experience can be as important as directly relevant experience – the key thing is taking learning from experience. I like people who have had some real work experience not just academic experience or voluntary positions. Getting a good work ethic and experience of team working from any job whether it be working in an office, shop or restaurant really helps. Having had experience of working with some kind of disadvantaged/disenfranchised group is really helpful.'

Of course, some recruiters use online sifts and assessment centres, so they seek to measure your competency without reading your application form. There are mixed views on this approach. Candidates can feel 'cheated' that their experience and background were not considered, and some team leaders can feel cut out of the process of recruiting their team members. However, it also means that recruitment is properly 'blind' and (subject to disproportionality being understood and avoided in the scoring systems) it can assist in increasing workforce diversity rather than recruiting people who look and sound like the panel.

Many successful registered forensic psychologists did not get their first trainee post or their second. Tenacity and resilience are important competencies that we look for in trainees, and sometimes, this is evident in the motivation to get a training post. The flip side of this is, if you receive feedback that indicates that perhaps this isn't the career for you, please listen, reflect and review. Such feedback may not be what you want to hear, but perhaps discuss it with those who know you best, reflect on the realities of the role and consider if this is right for you at this time. Perhaps it is something that you could come back to in a few years, or perhaps another direction, either in or outside of psychology, is the right one for you. Review this before a high financial or emotional commitment. We have met too many trainees who felt it wasn't necessarily 'for them', but they had invested so much into becoming a forensic psychologist that they were unable to see a way out, resulting in dissatisfaction, unhappiness and poor-quality services. If you find yourself in this position having already invested in this career path – for example, having completed an MSc – then all is not lost! As we have said a number of times throughout this book, forensic psychology training offers much more than just a route into forensic psychology. You will have acquired a number of transferable skills, including (but not exclusively) demonstrable critical thinking, an ability to link theory to practice and an understanding of practical skills needed when working with people. Academic and research skills are also part of any accredited postgraduate qualification in this field and offer a separate career trajectory too. You can exercise your creative skills and understanding to consider the transferable skills you have acquired and understand where might be best for you to apply them.

To sum it up perhaps quite starkly:

> *I see too many trainees who just won't take feedback; they don't trust the opinions and feedback from people such as myself who have been doing this job, supervising and supporting trainees for years. Sometimes you see quite soon that someone just isn't cut out for the job – but when you try and give them that feedback they don't want to hear it which then results in all sorts of grievances and messy results. Sometimes we get it wrong on recruitment, and then we have to deal with either poor quality of work, or trainees who just don't get it. We can train lots of skills, but some people will just never make a good forensic psychologist, like I would never make a good astronaut or ballet dancer, however hard I try.*

Not been put off yet? Brilliant. There is a bit of a theme emerging here – be committed, open, dedicated, organised, reflective, passionate and not unhealthily obsessed with serial killers. If this is you, you might make a great forensic psychologist.

Life as a Trainee

What is training like? The best way to get a feel for life as a trainee is to talk to those who have trained in recent years. Training routes have altered, with a shift from the historical BPS 'independent' route to the development of a number of university-based courses that provide the training experience. Here are some thoughts from several forensic psychologists who contributed whilst either in their training or upon recent completion, through a variety of methods, not only from those employed as trainees during their training years. We have already said something about the routes to qualification, and the following is a reflection from a recently graduated trainee.

> *'Training is like juggling lots of balls all at the same time, inside work and outside. You can be involved in lots of projects and assessments all at the same time as well as keeping a practice diary and working on submissions. Lots of time spent away training which takes some juggling with family commitments'.*

We talked earlier in the book about having the ability to gather and synthesise a range of information – when a trainee, you need to add in the multiple work and training strands that are needed and keep all the balls up in the air.

> *I think you need excellent planning skills to be successful, and flexibility when things don't quite go to plan. I am on a University route and really like the structured approach. I also like being attached to an academic institute and the benefits this*

> *brings with it (student discount, library facilities, recognised award at the end of training and graduation). Also with this route you have an academic supervisor as well as a clinical supervisor which I think works really well and is a nice balance'*

So for some, the additional structure of a university-led course can keep them on track, whereas the BPS route, for some, allows too much flexibility, as we see below. For others, of course, the flexibility is what makes the BPS route achievable.

> *'Before I undertook a trainee position it would have been useful had I known the expectations of what it would take to achieve the BPS qualification in a timely manner alongside the 'day job'. Working in an organisation as a trainee can be pretty full-on and I think I underestimated the scope of the day to day tasks easily encroaching onto my 'Chartership time'. I think it's fair to say that you need to be able to acknowledge the commitment you're prepared to 'put in' and work on your training portfolios within your own time. A handy tip to achieving this is to remember that the qualification is for your 'personal use', not your employer. If you later leave the organisation, you take your qualification with you, so it's unreasonable to think that you should be able to dedicate all your work-time to completing the qualification. Find a balance that works for you but be prepared to set yourself some goals to complete away from the office, keep focused on these, and you can achieve the BPS route in a timely manner. '*

Thinking back to the recruiter who wants a trainee to genuinely understand what the training route involves, this individual notes that:

> *'I think the job isn't necessarily what you think it is going to be before you start. There is much more report writing than I had imagined and this is a skill that takes time to develop. There is*

> *a great scope for variety and to specialise in different areas and get involved in different types of work; training, consultancy, research etc. I think I had really only thought about the prisoner assessment and intervention, without all of the other skills and areas that go alongside it'*

And here, we see someone trying to make explicit that what is asked for in terms of competencies is relevant for the job, not just for the interview:

> *'Through my previous experience of being a Trainee walking through the changing BPS route rules, and as a current Chartered Psychologist overseeing a number of teams, working in my capacity as training board chair and also via interviewing, selecting, working alongside and supervising Trainee's there are definitely key skills and strengths that spring to mind and I feel have been intrinsic in supporting and enabling individuals to progress and achieve with the qualification and a career within Forensic Psychology. I think Trainees or potential Trainees need to understand that the competencies highlighted during the recruitment and assessment process are an intrinsic part of the job. . . . and not just about getting the job! Making effective decisions, building capability for all, leading and communicating, collaborating and partnering, acting with integrity and showing drive and resilience are essential. I often find myself quoting or referring to these competencies within supervision sessions or when managing Trainees as they generally assist in making the points I need to. They really are an expectation of your daily role and it is evident that those individuals who truly understand and possess these competencies do progress and succeed. In terms of top tips, I would say be curious, look for and seek out opportunity, be self-driven and make things happen. Be flexible and always remember we work within a tough and ever changing landscape and always keep sight of the bigger picture and how you fit into this.*

Below, again, the practicalities – understanding the reality of training – we have an individual who completed the BPS route making two wishes to help future trainees:

> *'My first wish would have been to know the realities of the route, not just what the handbook or the BPS states. Things like how long it <u>actually</u> could take and how often people resubmit work. Whilst I don't regret doing the route and would've still pursued it if I had had this information I think it would have helped me start from a more realistic perspective. Related to the reality of the work, I would've also appreciated someone talking to me about how potentially this work could impact on me as a person both in good and not so good ways. I don't think that it is the sort of work that you can avoid being affected by.*
>
> *My second wish particularly now qualified would be to have known what the qualification would actually mean in terms of its level of achievement. Being told that we have studied to a doctorate level, it's just that we haven't got the related qualification (e.g. Dr/DForenPsy) to show for it, is all a bit confusing and frustrating at times. It feels like this explanation therefore means the work and achievement isn't fairly recognised or awarded accordingly. Also with the introduction of the university doctorate routes, my experience is that non psychologists tend to (at least initially) refer to the psychologist with the highest recognised qualification when seeking psychological input. And why wouldn't you – their qualification suggests a higher level of knowledge and skill.'*

Some trainees want to rush their training and get there as fast as they can. This is clearly understandable, but some context is below:

> *'My biggest observation of trainees (as a trainee and a qualified) is the attitude towards the training route. It can very easily become a tick box exercise, a means to an end, rather than it being a process and set of standards we should be using to develop our practice and competence as Forensic Psychologists. I think that the*

> *route itself and related administrative processes perpetuate this as well as the organisation at times, where the business need is about getting qualified Forensic Psychologists in post. What I would say to trainees is that you are not a different psychologist once you qualify and whilst it isn't about spending forever and a day reflecting on every minute experience, if the focus is too much on 'getting through' you are probably going to miss a lot of learning opportunities and therefore be a less competent psychologist. You are probably also going to become increasingly frustrated, disenchanted and resentful of the route along the way.'*

And more about understanding what you're entering into:

> *'In my experience, trainee psychologists that progress well, regardless of their training route, are those that spend time at the beginning of the process developing their understanding of the competencies required and how their role meshes with the competencies. Otherwise, their job becomes task focused, and they struggle to demonstrate or evidence their competency. Within my organisation, trainees come into post with a range of experience but often they will have gained some experience in the delivery of interventions. Although this helps their transition into a trainee role it is not the be all and end all. Being proactive in understanding the competencies, getting to grips with a Practice Diary and using the experience of colleagues around them and their supervisor, are as important.'*

The flip side of the 'taking time as a trainee' comments. This one seems about being organised and having insight into your developmental needs but not being afraid to push yourself.

> *'From my own experience of being a trainee, and also in supervising others, the key to training smoothly, broadly, and quickly*

> *is to look out for opportunities. Those trainees that tend to take longer to train, often have a more cautious approach (which of course isn't bad) but that are less willing to be flexible and take up new opportunities as they arise, and perhaps prefer to stay in a 'comfort zone'. Trainees that tend to do better also have excellent time management and planning skills. Employers have an expectation that trainees are flexible, and accountable for their time – multi-tasking and juggling a range of work, priorities and deadlines is part and parcel of a forensic psychologist's role and when basic planning skills are lacking makes progression tough for a trainee.'*

And the ones who are prepared and organised, with expectations clear:

> *'Having supervised a number of trainees, I have observed that those who make the 'best' progress on the training route are those who are able to 'hit the ground running', building on their existing skills and experience. It also helps when trainees are realistic about the level of work involved in completing all routes to qualification and recognise that they will need to spend their own time preparing submissions/Core Roles. Adaptability to change is also crucial when working as a trainee (and later as a qualified forensic psychologist) and those who manage to maintain their positivity and motivation under such conditions tend to do well. While needing to work within their limited remit and competencies, trainees who show initiative and are solution-focused in facing challenges are more likely to develop into sound practitioners. Openness to learning through training, supervision and reflective practice is essential, not just as a trainee, but for the remainder of your career as a forensic psychologist.'*

A lot of quotes, but some important key messages seem to be about understanding reality. Training in forensic psychology is tough, as it should be. This is a career where you will be responsible for making assessments, judgements and recommendations that will impact the lives of many – the client in front of you, their family, their victims, the wider public, the criminal justice agencies and many more. As well as your psychological skills and knowledge, you need a flexible approach to balancing your training demands versus organisational needs, with a good planning ability, with the pace of qualification being something which you need to 'own' and choose the pace by the level of your own time you are willing to invest. Do not be a passive recipient of training. Do not expect your employer to do all the running. Understand what is needed and work with your supervisor to find ways to achieve it.

There are a lot of competing demands; as a trainee, you are obviously focused on progressing your training, but you may also be employed by an organisation. These two demands do not have to be in conflict, but they can at times feel that way. It is important to think about how each and every activity relates to the competencies you are developing through your training and reflect on your experiences. We saw one of the earlier testimonials say that '*trainee psychologists that progress well, regardless of their training route, are those that spend time at the beginning of the process developing their understanding of the competencies required and how their role meshes with the competencies*'. This is where reflective practice comes to the fore. Understand that reflective practice is a process which is not a 'Bridget Jones' diary' type reflection of 'who or what I did today' but rather an essential mechanism for understanding the decisions made, the consequences, the rationale and the impact. Understanding such things is a key feature of being a good practitioner. There are a variety of reflective models available to help conceptualise the value and process of this approach, and learning from one's own experience following a reflective process is a key aspect of being a practitioner psychologist, which you should begin from the very start of your career and indeed continue until the very end.

Likewise, it is easy to push the training aside when focusing on your organisational job role. This happens all too often, with trainees reporting they have been busy 'doing their job' with no time to focus on their training portfolio when on the BPS route. After a while, it becomes harder to start the evidence gathering or to catch up. In our experience, it is often these people who take longer to qualify via the BPS route, as they become stuck in a place of 'training-stasis' – fairly experienced and indeed competent at a range of tasks as a trainee, but with no training route progression to show for it. It is easy to become disillusioned; to blame the employer, the supervisor and the BPS; and to note that more inexperienced trainees are 'overtaking' you as they have focused on their training in a way that you have not. Don't be one of these people – see every work and placement opportunity as a learning experience which needs to be captured, reflected upon and, where appropriate, included in your development portfolio. But also, reflect on the words of the testimonials who note that you need to maximise your learning and development, not just race through to your end goal. In the words of Gita Bellin, a pioneering management facilitator and coach, *'Success is a journey not a destination – half the fun is getting there'.* This is well worth remembering. And perhaps Lord of the Rings has advice for us too: *'it's the job that's never started that takes longest to finish'.*

Trainees who only think of their training are also doing themselves and the profession an injustice. When this happens, the client can at times seem to lose out and not be the central service user for whom we are there to work with. The trainee might view the service users (or employers) as simply the vehicle by which they train, demonstrate their competencies and achieve their personal goals. So, just as some put the job above training, others can put the training above the job – think carefully about this. You are working with service users to achieve your own personal qualification, but you are also there to provide a professional and ethical service, often to disadvantaged groups. They are not a vehicle for you to qualify or just material for your portfolios of evidence. It is vital to have the real service users at the centre of your thinking at all times – remember you are in a position of influence and your decisions can have a significant impact on the lives of others. Please never lose sight of this at any point in your career.

We often tell students or trainees that from the start of their careers, they must consider every action they undertake as a potential piece of evidence which can be brought before a court. This means that when faced with sometimes complex and conflicting information, this is understood and interpreted with consideration of the available theoretical literature – what is the latest thinking about a particular subject? How can the conflicting information be understood, and how must it be challenged? If you have the phrase 'defensible decisions' rattling around in your brain from the very beginnings of this line of work, then you should be secure in safe and ethical practice.

The Training

We've mentioned the BPS core roles previously. References to the 'training route' have been frequent with testimonials up to this point referencing a range of issues. So, we will turn our attention to the actual training routes available currently for becoming a forensic psychologist.

Unlike some other psychology domains, the routes to registration are a little confusing (to say the least)! In Chapter 2, we said that you needed to (1) get your MSc and (2) complete the supervised practice placement component. This is absolutely true, but the routes to achieving this are expanding.

Historically, the BPS training route was the way to become a forensic psychologist. Over recent years, additional routes have developed through universities and it is expected that they will continue to do so. These university routes are not, however, all the same! That would be far too simple.

There are practitioner doctorates in forensic psychology that cover both Stage 1 and Stage 2, and the BPS provides a Stage 2 QFP. Stage 2 involves a length of time (at least two years) spent in 'supervised practice'. This means that with support and guidance from one or more experienced colleagues, you can gain experience and develop the required skills to work as a forensic psychologist within a real-life context, for example, a prison or probation setting. A candidate may enrol on the QFP (Stage 2) having already produced evidence of demonstrating some of the competences required and may thus be eligible to apply for partial exemption.

The BPS Route

For those students who have successfully completed their accredited MSc in forensic psychology and plan to follow the BPS route, their next step will be completion of the *British Psychological Society Qualification in Forensic Psychology*. This requires candidates to enrol and then, over a period of time, to submit portfolios of written evidence to demonstrate competency development in relation to four core roles.

So, to enrol on the BPS route, you need

i)   Your MSc
ii) Some relevant experience and
iii) To be able to confirm that you have a supervisor who is prepared to attest to you being 'Chartership ready' and can work towards the core roles.

The BPS Qualification Board has undertaken an extensive review of the qualification – including engaging with stakeholders, focus groups and a root-and-branch review of the systems and processes with the BPS qualification route. This found that the core roles and competencies (as described below) were judged as remaining relevant. However, there were some clear issues – some individuals were spending far too long on this route, and some found it too onerous, inconsistent and confusing (as we have seen from quotes).

The review has sought to address these issues, and the 'new' or 'revised' qualification is not subject to the same problems, although any change brings with it teething and implementation issues. Changes have included aspects such as an induction process to help trainees properly understand what will be required of them in their submissions. Assessors use a more transparent marking criterion to improve consistency, and there is a time limit on completion, so you and your employer will know that in two, three or a maximum of four years, you will have achieved your goal. BPS registrars and assessors work closely to support candidates and provide ongoing feedback; submissions are streamlined for all trainees. Supervisors receive additional training and are supported with regular workshops delivered to assist with submission requirements. In short, these are very welcome and very necessary changes to the processes, all designed with the trainee in mind and the responsibility to their organisations.

As it stands, two exemplars (example pieces of work) for each core role need to be submitted, along with supporting evidence of competency development. This will need to include supporting evidence such as a practice diary detailing your reflections and learning in relation to daily tasks and a competence logbook detailing how you have developed and demonstrated your competence within each core role. This evidence must be signed off by your supervisor and is subsequently assessed by the lead assessor for that core role and ultimately the chief assessor for the qualification. You can take advantage of the range of CPD events facilitated by the BPS and advertised on their website. Events have included:

- Strategies to enhance resilience in critical occupations
- Forensic psychology research symposia
- QFP Stage 2 workshops

These four core roles have been mentioned briefly earlier. They are outlined below, along with feedback gained from the assessment team for each core role. This section draws heavily from Harrower's (2014) article in Forensic Update 114. In fact, this issue contains a number of useful articles about becoming a qualified psychologist. Two of the authors of this book were chief assessors for the BPS Qualification from 2008 to 2015 and one was Chair of the DFP Qualification Board, past Chair of the DFP Training Committee and also a past Chair of the DFP.

We have used the candidate handbook definitions with some further descriptions to bring them to life.

1. Core Role 1: Conducting applications and interventions

This Core Role is concerned with the cycle of assessment and intervention aimed at producing changes in individuals, operational or organisational functioning. Typically this involves identification, exploration and formulation of relevant issues and objectives; planning; achieving necessary working relationships; implementation and evaluation of efficacy. It can also involve the consideration and direction of other personnel. It always involves drawing upon a multi-faceted base of knowledge and skills in a systematic, analytical, responsive and ethical manner.

So, this core role is often seen as the 'bread and butter' work of forensic psychologists given the demand for services and, for that reason, is often the first core role for trainees to tackle from a portfolio of evidence perspective. We might also however think that this is the area which takes the longest to finesse and develop competence over time, not simply six months of practice compared to, for example, a training project or research evaluation. So it might be that an individual plans what they are going to do to meet this core role, but develops their skills and competence throughout their training. Although this core role is broken down into six specific competencies, essentially you are being asked whether or not you can demonstrate experience of working face to face with service users. You will have to comment on whether you can assess challenging people, whether you have experience of doing this in a variety of settings – in prison, court or the community, for example – also whether you have been able to work with them both 1:1 and in a group. This really is the basics of forensic psychology, and you can demonstrate it by showing what kind of assessments you have done and your skills of formulation (i.e. essentially using your psychological skills and knowledge to work out 'what's going on' with the service user) as well as evidencing the ongoing work or 'interventions' you have conducted. You will have to comment on how effective your intervention has been and also consider whether your measure of efficacy is reliable or not.

The core role is broken down into six specific competencies that are assessed, outlined in the handbook below:

'. . .

1.1 Establishing requirements for, and the benefits of, applications/ interventions

1.2 Planning of applications/interventions

1.3 Establishing, developing and maintaining working relationships

1.4 Implementing applications/interventions

1.5 Directing implementation of applications/interventions carried out by others.

1.6 Evaluating results of applications/interventions . . .'

Over time, we have amassed feedback on the BPS route;
<u>Identified strengths in CR1 submissions</u> have included:

- Use of theory to underpin the assessments and interventions
- Good choices of exemplar projects
- Attention to ethical issues and to anonymity
- Evidence of good practice in working with other professional colleagues

<u>Identified weaknesses in CR1 submissions</u> have included:

- Not providing enough evidence of the candidate's own contribution from a forensic psychology perspective
- Not providing enough signposting or a clear explanation of how the evidence provided clearly demonstrates the competency
- More evidence is needed for better planning and use of the relevant literature
- Recognition that evaluation is an integral component of assessment and intervention work and must be factored into the initial planning

2. Core Role 2: Research

CR2 is concerned with the design, conduct, analysis and evaluation of applied psychological research in forensic settings. Typically this involves the generation of ideas for specific research; the formulation of testable research questions; the definition of parameters and resources required for research; the planning, preparation and design of psychological research investigations and the identification of appropriate research tools; negotiating for access and resources to conduct research; the collection of data; appropriate analysis of research data and appropriate interpretation and evaluation of results; the formulation of recommendations based on the outcomes of research.

Historically, it is CR2 which trainees like least and often leave till last. But showing that you understand how to conduct good research and that you have the skills to understand what 'good research' looks like (and can therefore discriminate between good and bad research) is essential to a forensic psychologist and a skill you will need to rely on throughout your career. You have to remember that forensic psychology is a science after all and exercising those scientist muscles means demonstrating your research ability. Good research is not just lab-based, theoretical and boring, communicated only through pursed lips or mellifluously long words. Good research – and the kind you need to demonstrate here – involves a process of understanding why it needs to be done (the 'gap' in the literature), considering how you can answer the question and devising a methodology that tests useful questions. This is a human profession and the results of good research can really benefit our understanding of human behaviour. It is the obligation of every forensic psychologist to try and contribute to the body of knowledge we use to work in our field, and so, although some trainees can view this as frankly tedious and unpleasant, it is important that those trainees reflect on why they feel this way and try to remember the 'bigger picture'. The reason this is here is that it is important, it can contribute to really helping people, and it safeguards the integrity of our profession. So devising a sound, robust and ethical research plan is really important, as well as executing it and reporting on it in the most transparent way possible. Having a good supervisor to guide you through this process will make all the difference! It can be fun. . . . We promise! Sort of.

This core role is comprised of three specific competencies that are assessed:

'*2.1 Designing psychological research activities*
2.2 Conducting research activities
2.3 Analysing and evaluating psychological research data'

Some questions candidates may want to ask themselves before submission of the CR2 include:

- Is an organisational need being met?
- Is there a critical literature review, and does it justify the research question?

- Is the hypothesis or research question clearly stated?
- Is the method sufficiently well described to be understandable and replicable?
- Are reliable and valid measures used?
- Does the analysis follow the research report format?
- Is the dissemination appropriate for non-technical stakeholders as well as psychologists?
- Is the data collection ethical?

Experience shows that many trainees do CR2 pieces of work, which are far too ambitious – or sometimes insufficiently forensic. Your exemplar plan will shape what you can achieve when you submit it for approval – but they are unlikely to tell you if it's too big! That's where a good supervisor comes in.

3. Core Role 3: Communicating psychological knowledge and advice to other professionals

CR3 is concerned with giving information, advice, guidance and feedback to personnel, agencies and organisations to enable effective problem-solving and decision-making, formulation and implementation of policy and practice. The emphasis is upon using appropriate communication skills to exert a constructive and psychologically based influence within current systems. It is this emphasis on communication that distinguishes it from CR1, although in practice these roles are often complementary.

As a forensic psychologist, you will be looked to as an expert in your field. Once you get over the inevitable 'imposter syndrome' that many of us still feel, the reality dawns that you are, in fact, in a position where you have gained knowledge, skills and experience which can be helpful to your fellow professionals. It can also be helpful on a wider scale – either through influencing organisational or wider policy. So, developing and demonstrating the skill to be a 'consultant' is crucial given the platform you are likely to have in your professional career. You might be giving evidence in court, a parole process, a tribunal or acting as an organisational consultant to support service users and peers. All of these things demonstrate your skills in communication and as a consultant, and you will come to rely on these skills throughout your working life. This core role is comprised of seven specific competencies that are assessed:

> '*3.1 Promoting awareness of the actual and potential contribution of applied psychological services*
>
> *3.2 Providing psychological advice to assist and inform problem solving and decision-making*
>
> *3.3 Providing psychological advice to aid the formulation of policy and its implementation*
>
> *3.4 Preparing and presenting evidence in formal settings*
>
> *3.5 Responding to informal requests for psychological information*
>
> *3.6 Providing feedback to clients*
>
> *3.7 Understanding organisational and systemic issues of relevance to the practice of applied psychologists*'

We sometimes call CR3 'consultancy' as the heart of the work is in providing expert psychological knowledge and advice to others. This is what psychologists do all the time; the trick is to capture it for a submission.

Things to think about in CR3 submissions have included:

- Make links between literature and practice
- Demonstrate how the work contributes to policy formulation and practice
- Ensure evaluation is thought about
- Explicit reference to psychological evidence needs to be made

4. Core Role 4: Training other professionals in psychological skills and knowledge

Core Role 4 is concerned with imparting to other professionals' knowledge and skills where there is an important psychological component. In addition, many psychologists work in settings where improving job performance of other staff is a major part of their professional service.

This is different from core role 3 because here we are considering training and not just consultancy. The question for a trainee to reflect on in this core role is whether they have been able to undertake a clear process to develop helpful training for other professionals. For example, have they conducted a training needs analysis (TNA), have they consulted appropriately, have they developed their own materials, and have they delivered the training, reflected on feedback and then been able to improve subsequent training? Being able to take feedback with humility and understanding is an important part of being a forensic psychologist – it crops up everywhere. This is a good opportunity to demonstrate your approach to integrating feedback into delivery. The individual components of this core role are:

> '4.1 *Identifying and analysing needs to improve or prepare for job performance in specific areas.*
>
> 4.2 *Planning and design of training and development programmes.*
>
> 4.3 *Implementation of training and development programmes.*
>
> 4.4 *Planning and implementation of assessment procedures for evaluating training and development programmes.'*

We have seen some great CR4 submissions, and the sort of things you might want to think about include:

- Make sure you make use of TNA methodology to explain, structure and plan the work, including elements such as project risk assessment and the obtaining of agreement from others
- Have evidence-based aims and objectives, noting the significance to the wider work environment
- Show a demonstration of how the training was implemented, taking into account issues of resourcing
- Show your planning and implementation of appropriate assessment systems
- Have a structured evaluation review and report, designed and reviewed with the agreement of others and showing both strengths and areas for improvement

For more on this, read Harrower, J. (2014) 'Becoming a Qualified Forensic Psychologist', *Forensic Update Annual Compendium*, BPS.

The content of the BPS training route is flexible. Flexibility is the ability to adapt to current employment opportunities and to your own work-life fit or domestic needs, yet this can also have potential difficulties for trainees in accessing opportunities to undertake work related to particular competencies at the appropriate time.

The BPS Stage 2 qualification currently has a single cost of just over £8K, with additional costs depending on your circumstances (e.g. if you want previous experience to be considered). There may also be some additional costs, such as supervisor costs, depending on where/ how/with whom you complete the training.

A positive relationship between a trainee and their supervisor is crucial. This is because the supervisor must guide their trainee in relation to improving their practice and demonstrating competence. The supervisor also has to sign off all the trainee's work. Providing critical as well as constructive feedback and appropriate levels of support is crucial to success and helps to develop good practice. You need to expect that your supervisor will at times be critical. Constructive, I would hope, but their aim is to help your progression whilst maintaining safe and effective service to the service user.

On completion of the BPS route, you are eligible to apply for registered status with the HCPC and use the protected title 'forensic psychologist'. You are also eligible for Chartered status of the BPS and full membership of the Division of Forensic Psychology in the BPS. You may use the term 'CPsychol'.

The BPS currently offers two-, three- and four-year routes on their qualification; which one of these is best for you would need careful consideration as to how much time is actively spent on developing your portfolio, the requirements of your employer/placement and the supervision demands. The two-year route is challenging but possible!

University Routes

There are *practitioner doctorates and professional qualification programmes in forensic psychology offered by some universities,* and it is worth checking the BPS website for updated lists of providers. Some examples current at the time of writing are detailed below. On completion of these routes, you are eligible to apply for registered status with the HCPC and use the protected title 'forensic'. You are also eligible for Chartered status of the BPS and full membership of the Division of Forensic Psychology in the BPS. You may use the term

'CPsychol'. You may also refer to yourself as 'Dr', and it is a useful route to explore when the time comes. It would be a good idea to speak to qualified forensic psychologists to gain an informed view of people's experiences on these programmes.

Trainee Case Studies:

A batch of trainees undertaking the University Registration Route

---

Case Study 1: Trainee Psychologist University Route

Q. Did you transfer over from BPS route? If so what's the advantages of the university route to you?

I joined the university route to registration in October 2013. Prior to this I had been on the BPS Stage 2 route for a number of years but had not submitted any work or made much progress.

Q. How are you finding the university route in comparison?

I find the structure of the course fits well with my personal learning style. The Standards of Proficiency and placement handbook clearly outline what needs to be evidenced, and how this can be best achieved in the various submissions. The three-monthly submission deadlines give me a target to work towards that has kept me focused with my training submissions.

Q. What do you find works well?

Having a clinical and academic supervisor is helpful as I know who to ask for which type of support. I also find it encouraging that they both agree their feedback before our tri-partite meetings. When I was on the BPS route I often saw colleagues receive conflicting feedback from their BPS assessors, which seemed to be confusing and it put me off submitting as I was unsure what I needed to do. Access to the provider's library and online archives is helpful.

Q. What do you find difficult/a challenge?

The only negative point is that some of the workshops I have attended have been quite basic. This feedback has been given to the Course Director and I am aware that they have made subsequent changes. I like the provision of 'peer mentors' too, as there is an opportunity to liaise directly with other trainees on the course.

Q. What tips or advice would you give to others on this route or considering it?

I would say to speak to the Course Director and ask to speak to trainees already on the route for an idea of what is involved. Ultimately, it's worth speaking to their supervisor and the Course Director to discuss individual circumstances.

Case Study 2: Trainee Psychologist University Route

Q. Did you transfer over from BPS route? If so what's the advantages of the University route to you?

No. I completed stage one (MSc) of the BPS route. Due to the flexibility of the university route it allowed me to start (self-funded) before securing a trainee post. Whilst in a reduced hours Intervention Facilitator post I was able to volunteer one day per week at a Therapeutic Community and get started. Although it was on a part-time basis so progress was slow, at least I was able to get started and it helped me to secure a full-time trainee psychologist post.

Q. How are you finding the university route?

I started at the very beginning of the course setting up. As such the route was still finding its feet. I have found that over the last few years there has been lots of learning and improvement to the route resulting in a much clearer direction of what submissions should look like, what needs to be included etc.

Q. What do you find works well?

You have an Academic Supervisor as well as your Clinical Supervisor, I find this really helpful; two different perspectives but working towards the same aim. Whilst there is flexibility about how you meet the needs of the qualification from your job role there is structure to the course. Recently the University has added podcasts for each of the reflective reports that can be accessed online. It is possible to qualify in two years if you work hard and stick to your targets.

Q. What do you find difficult/a challenge?

As the University is far from where I'm located, I initially felt quite remote and isolated. However there are lots of more trainees now coming onto the route which really helps for support.

Q. What tips or advice would you give to others on this route or considering it?

Do your practice diary every day! Break it down, set mini goals, to achieve your overall goal (getting qualified). It's a marathon not a sprint.

Case Study 3: Trainee Psychologist University Route

Q. Did you transfer over from BPS route? If so what's the advantages of the HCPC route to you?

Yes. I transferred over from the BPS Stage 2 route having first successfully passed Core Role 1 which meant I could use this as prior accredited learning for gaining extra credits.

Q. How are you finding the university route?

There are a lot of similarities, and the demands and depth of the work is the same between the two routes. However the advantages I have found is the clarity and transparency of what is required. I am able to (and have) contacted the course director for anything I need clarity on. Access to resources (i.e. electronic journals, books etc.) is amazing with it being a university course.

Q. What do you find works well?

I feel through this route I will become a better clinician as there is an emphasis on demonstrating ethical and professional practice on a daily basis, and we get regular feedback on our 'performance'. Your CS being one of your assessors I think is also a big advantage for both parties – more investment in each other. Having regular contact with my academic supervisor is also really useful for clarity and accountability – I felt the BPS was faceless and I could not speak to somebody if I needed some help.

Q. What do you find difficult/a challenge?

There is more emphasis on theory and research (which runs through everything) so there is a lot of study outside of work. However I feel this is more manageable as work gets handed in every 3 months – this makes it easier and more manageable with work/life commitments.

Q. What tips or advice would you give to others on this route or considering it?

Mentally prepare yourself for the amount of study you need to do outside of work. Familiarise yourself with the HCPC Standards of Proficiency (so you have an understanding of what is expected of you). Speak to people on the route. Finally – enjoy it, this is a great opportunity to hone your skills and become the practitioner you want to be.

Case Study 4: Trainee Psychologist University Route

Q. Did you transfer over from BPS route? If so what's the advantage of the University route to you?

Yes, I transferred over. The main advantage for me was having a set structure and deadlines that are non-negotiable as this suits me better and provides me with clear and set goals to work towards.

Q. How are you finding the University route?

I have just submitted my first piece of work and I'm awaiting feedback. The process of submitting work is very similar to the BPS route but the amount of work involved can be tailored to the individual. I submitted the equivalent of ½ of CR1. I am still in the process of understanding the Standards of Proficiency that we need to evidence throughout the University route and will know more about expectations from the route after receiving feedback.

Q. What do you find works well?

Having a set deadline with clear, agreed expectations of what is to be submitted is helpful. When on the BPS route it was often the case that a submission target was pushed back due to other priority work which meant I didn't need to push myself to submit. As the deadlines are agreed in advance, and there is the influence of an external academic supervisor, this is not possible and therefore I approach it more like a University course in terms of having to meet the deadlines.

Q. What do you find difficult/a challenge?

The amount of work involved in the university route is equivalent to the BPS route and therefore there are still challenges finding time to keep up with practice diaries etc.

> **Q. What tips or advice would you give to others on this route or considering it?**
>
> Become familiar with the standards of proficiency relevant to the HCPC forensic practitioner role in advance as this is the main learning curve in the initial phases. For those new to the role of trainee try to gain as much experience of different risk assessment tools, delivery models (interventions) and work with offenders as this will put them in the best position to start submitting pieces of work as soon as possible upon starting the route.

Words from Some Qualified Psychologists

Cast Study 5: Forensic Psychologist

How long have you been qualified and a Chartered Psychologist for?

I Chartered in Sept 2014. I submitted my final Core Role at three years but it failed twice so I passed at around four years.

Q. What advice or tips would you give to someone currently on Stage 2 of the BPS route?

Set yourself small achievable goals that are easier to work towards. Consider your attitude towards the process – if you start to feel as though the process is becoming a burden it can lead to feeling resentful of the process. Remind yourself of why you started this training and what you want to achieve.

Take ownership of the work – see each project as a new way to develop and learn. Set yourself 'rules' that you are happy to work with (regarding remote working in your own time). I set 'one evening per week, and one weekend day'. That way I could be flexible as to which days, and I could keep a work-life balance. Remember, being a good qualified psychologist is not about getting your CRs in quickly, it's about having the knowledge, competence and experience to back it up.

Q. What helped you to remain motivated and solution focused?

Recognise that dips in motivation may happen and set small goals during this time to get things done so it feels like you are still achieving. Get support from your supervisor and submitting work gives you a boost to work towards that goal.

Not seeing this route as something that my workplace 'owes me', for example, I'm 'owed time in work'. It was my choice to do the work and it's my career path.

Crucial: Feeling ok about completing work in my own time and seeing this as part of the process rather than begrudging this.

Q. What should people on Stage 2 try and avoid to stay on track?

Avoid getting behind on practice diaries – this can really affect morale. Avoid getting bogged down with negative feelings about the process, it is tough, but it's a career choice and one that you have chosen.

Case Study 6: Forensic Psychologist

Q. How long did it take you to become a Chartered Psychologist?

To complete stage 2, it took eight years. It took me four years to submit my first core role.

Q. What advice or tips would you give to someone currently on Stage 2 of the BPS route?

I think I would advise them to try and focus on the core role as a whole, and to consider how the individual piece of work (lit review etc.) fits into that. This also helps with completing the practice diary as it helps to reflect on what the work is for, how it fits in and how it could be done differently.

Q. What helped you to remain motivated and solution focused?

I think a major factor for me was having a supervisor who understood me and how I worked. We developed a good working relationship and could reflect on how I worked, the things that triggered off my weirdness (anxiety, stress and inability to focus) and how I could get over that and focus on the work. We set clear deadlines and prioritised these, so I could achieve each milestone. I think my supervisor was a huge factor in making progress, and believing that I could.

Q. What should people on Stage 2 try and avoid to stay on track?

I think it's important that they try and avoid getting stuck in a negative thought cycle. By this, I include avoid listening to the horror stories about Stage 2!

I think it is useful to think about the structure of each core role, and to consider what pieces of work they can complete to demonstrate the competencies. I think there is also benefit in seeing submissions as progression so that some people may be able to consider that the feedback the submission will offer them will be helpful in them progressing, in case the submission doesn't get through the first time, frustrating as that may be.

Case Study 7: Forensic Psychologist

Q. How long have you been qualified and a Chartered Psychologist for?

I've been Chartered nearly two years now. It took me three years to qualify so it can be done! I loved it (rare I know!) so take quite a practical view on it.

Q. What advice or tips would you give to someone currently on Stage 2 of the BPS route?

Enjoy it, you are developing a fabulous career. Set goals and keep on track with them using the quarterly supervision plans as a way of setting targets and regularly review during supervision. Accept that it's not meant to be easy – we are working with a complicated client group so need to be good at what we do! Nobody enjoys practice diaries but make sure they are specific and clearly signpost developing competence – don't waffle!!

Appreciate that the training costs the organisation a lot of money – think of it as if it was your own money, that way you will become focused – nobody wants to spend more than they need to and this is the same for Psych Services budget!

You need to do work in your own time. Just like at University. Just like Doctors revising for exams. Just like teachers marking work. Just like the supervisors who read your practice diaries. That's just how it is.

Q. What helped you to remain motivated and solution focused?

Use supervision constructively rather than complain about office politics. The attitude of go hard or go home and a promise to myself of a mulberry bag at the end of it! A group of us had study club one Saturday every month to support & help each other. Create opportunities – they don't always fall onto your desk. The post qualification opportunities can be amazing so why would you want to put that off!

Q. What should people on Stage 2 try and avoid to stay on track?

Procrastination, writing your 6th study plan is still not getting you closer to doing the work. Just do it.

Getting sucked into negativity about the process. Pointless.

Case Study 8: Forensic Psychologist

Q. How long have you been qualified and a Chartered Psychologist for?

I Chartered in 2011 and it took me four years.

Q. What advice or tips would you give to someone currently on Stage 2 of the BPS route?

Keep on top of practice diaries (do not get behind!) & keep on top of all other paperwork.

Use supervision emails within your PD to capture the time spent in supervision & attend supervision with an agenda, you should set the supervision not your supervisor (take responsibility for this). Join or set-up peer groups which encourage the sharing of feedback from assessors and helpful tips/advice; ask to see other peoples examples of work that was submitted to understand what a CR 'looks like'; think outside the box, you are training to be a psychologist not a prison psychologist so scope out areas to develop your practice.

Q. What helped you to remain motivated and solution focused?

A peer supervision group we set up across the region. I also had personal motivation as I was at a stage in my life when I had got married and we were considering a family but I did not want to go off on maternity leave and have to return to complete the training route.

Q. What should people on Stage 2 try and avoid to stay on track?

As mentioned above, avoid getting behind on diaries and change your mind-set on the purpose of this task – see the bigger picture with diaries rather than seeing them as a 'chore' and pointless.

Avoid unhelpful conversations with colleagues who have taken a long time, everyone's journey is different.

Finally, avoid saying 'I just have to write it up'; this is a huge task so don't make it sound like it's not and get it done.

Case Study 9: Forensic Psychologist

Q. How long did it take you to get qualified as a Chartered Psychologist?

It took about 5–6 years to gain Chartership.

Q. What advice or tips would you give to someone currently on Stage 2 of the BPS route?

Spend time really getting to know the competencies for each core role and keep refreshing over them. This will help you to more readily identify what CR's the task being done on a daily basis fit under and how you are continuously working towards the qualification.

When feeling motivated, go with it and complete as much work as possible. Also accept that your motivation may dip at points but then identify what is causing the dip & ways of increasing it again.

Take opportunities to gather information and network wherever you can. If possible try to go to a conference like the BPS trainee or the DFP conference, or Psychology Post Graduate (Psypag) conferences. Apply to present your work at a conference.

Rather than seeing your core role work as box ticking or hurdles to get over, focus on the opportunities to add strings to your bow.

Q. What helped you to remain motivated and solution focused?

Try to write up submissions as you're going along. This is easiest for CR2 and 4 whereby there is a set process to follow. This makes compiling the submission at the end easier to do. Try to submit a CR as soon as possible/competent. This will reinforce the process that needs to be taken and help to motivate once one CR has passed. Discuss with Co-ordinating Supervisor which CR's best fit with the work being undertaken for business needs and this should also be reflected in the quarterly plan.

Q. What should people on Stage 2 try and avoid to stay on track?

Don't try to focus on too many CR's at once. Plan which you want to submit next and work towards it by breaking down the CR into manageable tasks. Don't underestimate how long it takes to compile a submission <u>and</u> how long the supervision process may take and plan for it. If you receive feedback that a submission has not shown competency, then reflect on it and where possible work to address the issues sooner rather than later and resubmit.

Some Common Concerns

We have tried to make it as clear as possible what the options are, but we often find that the training remains difficult to understand, and some worry whether the registered route is 'good enough' due to not having

Chartered status. To reiterate, HCPC registration is the only legal requirement for a practitioner psychologist in any domain. You may hear some
psychologists talk about this as the 'minimum requirement' to practise
and then say that Chartership is the 'gold standard'. So, the ability to call
yourself a 'forensic psychologist', which is the protected title, comes with
HCPC registration, and you will automatically be HCPC registered if
you become Chartered through any of the routes described in this book.
But it is possible to just be HCPC registered and not be Chartered. It is
this which some will describe as the 'minimum legal requirement'.

So, is Chartered status necessary, or is it at least helpful? The BPS
describes the title of *Chartered Psychologist* as the benchmark of professional recognition for psychologists and reflects the highest standards
of psychological knowledge and expertise. If a professional is Chartered, it provides a mark of experience, competence and reputation for
anyone looking to employ, consult or learn from a psychologist.

The title and qualification (CPsychol) are legally recognised and can
only be conferred by the BPS, which has national responsibility in the
United Kingdom for the development, promotion and application of
psychology for the public good.

Qualifying for Chartered membership status is a significant achieve-
ment and requires evidence of:

- High levels of academic attainment;
- Periods of supervised practice and applied experience;
- A commitment to lifelong learning;
- An engagement with the broader issues facing the profession.

These foundations are further strengthened by the BPS Member Conduct
Rules and Codes of Ethics and Conduct, which all Chartered Psycholo-
gists must follow. Once they have been formally approved by the BPS,
Chartered Psychologists may use the letters CPsychol after their name.

The BPS would say this, as since the introduction of the HCPC as the
regulator and register of psychologists, the role of the BPS has, some feel,
become less clear and they are promoting Chartership as highly valuable.
However, registered not Chartered does not mean that an individual is
any less competent or experienced. Some psychologists choose not to
be a BPS member, despite being eligible. But for those of us who have
been developed with the BPS as our professional body, we are used to

it and generally, we tend to retain it. Some would argue that there is value in being part of a professional body – both in terms of transparency in standards and in building networks and finding colleagues who have had similar professional experiences. It is an approach used by other professions – for example, medicine – but you will have to make your own decision over the value of a professional body to you. As authors of this book, all of us have been very involved with the BPS and support the value of a professional body, but that is true for us in our experiences and as we write.

Potentially as training routes continue to develop in the future, this may become less relevant for others, but it is the duty of the professional body to remain current and demonstrate value to its members. The BPS does this for forensic psychology through the high demand of ethics, standards and quality with oversight over all vocational qualification programmes for forensic psychology, including 'Chartership'. Not being Chartered does limit some access to relevant circles; for example, the Division of Forensic Psychology is the professional body for forensic psychology and is particularly targeted to the interests of those who hold a BPS qualification in the field. Of course, the landscape may change and Chartership become more important, particularly if the new route is favoured by employers and supervisors with Chartered status are required!

There are various other sources of information out there. The BPS trainee forum is one of these, but you need to be on the route to access it. Other blogs exist which can be useful sources of support and information if the person who writes and moderates them knows the information well enough!

For example:

- Forensicpsychtrainees.blogspot.com
- Thestudentroom.co.uk

There are also some interesting non-UK-based forums out there – interesting content, but try not to get confused with UK and other jurisdictions' legislation, terminology and training routes/qualifications!

- Forensicpsychologyonline.com

Several university providers also run blogs for MSc and Stage 2 course students.

Starting Out – Entering the Work Environment

5

Working as a Psychologist for the First Time

Your academic requirements are in place, you have successfully nego-
tiated job interviews and whichever training route you needed to
subscribe to, and you are about to enter the workplace. This may be
as a forensic psychologist in training (trainee forensic psychologist),
or it may be that you are now qualified. Well done – and don't be
scared – we're very pleased to welcome you to what we think is the
best job there is! We will deal with each separately, although there
is, of course, significant overlap (and, of course, with the previous
chapters on training when an employee).

Starting Out as a Trainee

The training route you have chosen needs adhering to; we won't
rehearse these again, but there are a range of other aspects to consider.
Some find that the job, quite simply, is not what they expected. This
can particularly be the case in those early days when the trainee may feel
they should be able to work directly with service users, yet their management prefers a slower start. It is important to remember that there
are a whole range of considerations here: your experience, your competence, your confidence, your awareness of the environment in which
you will be operating, your own and organisational safety and security,
and the rights and needs of service users, to name but a few. This may
be as a trainee but also as a qualified psychologist – it's really the same

DOI: 10.4324/9781315675831-5

in any new job – you need to familiarise yourself with your environment and the expectations and demands.

What to wear? We post no apologies for including this here. There are a number of issues to consider. It is important to present as professional, yet appropriate, for the environment in which you work. There is literature relating to the impressions that dress can create (the HCPC monograph regarding professionalism may be useful reading here; this does not relate to psychology but has a number of relevant points contained within)[13] and what we know about first impressions is that once formed, they can be hard to shift. So think about how you want to be perceived. An overly formal and/or expensive attire may be highly professional but might not be the best for rapport building with vulnerable and/or socially deprived others. Yet being too casual may provide the impression of insufficient care or professionalism. Think also about the environment you will be working in. The dress code is usually set within organisations, even if in very loose terms. So consider, just because the dress code does not explicitly say 'no flip-flops' or 'no crop tops' or 'no ripped jeans', what does wearing such items say about you to the other staff and service users? What is the potential impact of such items on your own safety and security? Recently, staff in one forensic setting were reminded not to wear a particular style of scarf when on the units due to the potential for such items making strangulation an easier task.

Service Users: Perhaps one of the most difficult things we see is psychologists, who regard themselves as agents of change, being either unaware of, or defensive about, the perception of some service users and the power imbalance implicit in their role. Within the forensic field, very many of our individual service users are not there by choice. Forensic psychology requires a different approach than clinical or counselling; whilst they may also focus on risk for an individual client, we do so whilst considering risk from multiple (client) perspectives. Whilst helping the individual reduce that risk is also an important part of our role, we are sometimes seen as agents of the state/organisation.[14] This conflict between often our own perceived role and that of others can be difficult to come to terms with.[15] Those who do not concern themselves with such things and are perfectly at ease with being an 'agent of the state' may be better suited to certain forensic roles where their personal impact on service users is reduced or where their remit is very well defined in that way (e.g. police work). Crewe (2007) provides what can be uncomfortable reading for some in the Prison Service, highlighting how specialist staff such as psychologists are perceived by some prisoners:

specialist staff were seen as part of an extensive, repressive and increasingly powerful network of disciplinary knowledge whose influence reflected a key transformation in the nature as well as the location of penal power. Many prisoners viewed psychological expertise with particular suspicion, identifying it as judgmental, objectifying and deeply insidious – no longer concerned with prisoner welfare as much as public protection.

This feedback can be hard to hear when an individual genuinely tries hard to assist prisoners, but it also provides a useful mirror to hold up to reflect on one's own practice and beliefs. Of course, public protection is a core part of the role of many forensic psychologists and should not be ignored, but we should not be defensive when we hear criticism; we should review and improve.

Clients are frequently not meeting with forensic psychologists on a voluntary basis and may have no or very limited opportunity to direct their assessment and treatment.

Informed Consent

Forensic psychologists regularly work with a different approach to confidentiality than other branches of psychology or health professions. This may mean that service users tend to withhold more information than in many therapeutic settings, which places the psychologist in the role of 'investigator', which can serve to further reinforce the belief of the psychologist as a non-helping agent of the state. Substantial rights and liberties are often at risk in forensic matters, and because the methods and procedures of forensic practitioners can be complex and may not be anticipated by the recipients of the services, forensic psychologists must always strive to inform service users about the nature and parameters of the services, including the advantages and disadvantages of consenting to engage.

Where consent is not given, the psychologist has a number of choices. These involve waiting and trying again, ensuring that the information was properly targeted at the individual given their background (perhaps their learning needs). Otherwise, they may simply report to the original party that the client has declined to engage, or they may decide to complete an assessment (for example) based purely on the documentation available to them. There is no wrong or right answer here; it will depend on the circumstances of the case. What should be considered is the importance of language. The service user may have declined; s/he may have done so vociferously. It may be better to describe this and their reasons for declining in clear terms rather than using language such as 'refused'. They may well have refused, but the more emotive term is unnecessary and may say more about your own feelings on the matter.

Staff Attitudes: From your training, you are probably aware of the different opinions those staff colleagues you work with may hold towards your profession and towards you both as a member of that profession and as an individual. Put simply, some staff groups do not value psychology. Their focus may be on security and safety, and they may believe that resources would be better directed in those areas than into psychology services. This will depend very much on the organisational culture and explicit aims and values of that organisation.

A First Qualified Post

Newly qualified psychologists are ready to work as autonomous professionals, responsible for their own professional activities. This can, for some, be quite a shock. You will have gone from your every move being scrutinised by those professionally responsible for your practice to now being expected to know your trade and go it alone. For some, perhaps particularly for those who have been trainees for many years, this can be a significant change to their working patterns which may or may not be welcomed. Some still expect others to review their work before submission. Others are very quick to point out that they are now independent practitioners and are responsible for their own practice. I would suggest that somewhere in the middle is best for safe and effective practice! You are now an independent practitioner. You are individually registered with the HCPC and are now held responsible for your own practice.

That means that you cannot expect others to take responsibility for you, but nor should you be thrown out of any support structures to help you.

Perhaps also for some, they achieve registered status and actually . . . not that much changes – they simply don't receive the same level of supervision as before. This can be quite an anticlimax when you have worked so hard to achieve something, but apart from perhaps a promotion or more money, many aspects of the role remain the same. Be aware that this is how it might feel to help manage your expectations!

Key Skills a Forensic Psychologist Develops

So once you are registered as a forensic psychologist and working, your training and development don't stop there. You will ensure that you seek to develop your skills, partly as you may be included in an HCPC CPD audit and partly because we are all learning as research and evidence develop and as our own practices either improve or need refreshing. New assessment and intervention techniques develop; new research needs reading. A few core skills which may seem simple are outlined below.

Interviewing Offenders

The ability to engage with offenders is a key skill for a forensic psychologist. This is relevant, particularly in the interviewing process. A forensic psychologist needs to be able to build rapport and seek to suspend judgement yet be very clear as to the outcome of the interview and the information required without being overly formulaic and, for example, following their interview aims to the letter and therefore missing other cues or information. The aim of the interview, as with any interview, is to gain information. What is often the case is that you are seeking to gather information that potentially the interviewee does not wish to share, that they may have difficulties recalling accurately and that you then need to take away to properly review and formulate your thoughts around the case.

You need to think about your own presentation and develop insight and knowledge into your own and more general 'bias' and thinking errors (read Kahneman for some excellent background on this) and also how aspects such as your gender, age, ethnicity and background can impact the interview process.

Hargie and Tourish (2000) describe five key features of effective communication skills. They refer to a 'seamless' process which flows with ease, conveying confidence and knowledge whilst simultaneously listening, responding to verbal and nonverbal cues whilst also taking notes and focusing on the direction of travel without appearing formulaic. Easy, right?

These are skills which can be developed and honed in order to meet the requirements of each interview. Motivational interviewing (MI) techniques are the starting point often for psychology staff in all walks of life. MI was developed by two British psychologists, William Miller and Steven Rollnick, based on their work in addiction. It is a client-centred counselling approach which aims to enhance motivation to change and support clients in setting concrete goals. We won't get into details here, but there is significant literature around MI, which is worth reading due to its general application to forensic work.[16]

You will also be working with other psychologists and will be able to benefit from collective discussions with other professional colleagues in relation to individual offenders and preferred ways of working. It is worth remembering that some other staff groups may have a different view of offenders or may have different agendas and may also be somewhat sceptical of forensic psychologists' assessments or interventions. However, good multidisciplinary working involves listening to a range of perspectives. The observations of others through different lenses and their experience are important, and a collaborative approach can be very effective in getting a full picture of an individual. For example, how someone presents to you in an interview is not necessarily how they present to staff on a wing, or in education or a workshop or to their caseworker.

Challenges and Issues

The client: An individual must identify the lead client, clarify roles, present data objectively and avoid dual relationships. We contend that this is a greater challenge in forensic practice – particularly when in criminal justice, not health settings, around confidentiality and maintaining relationships.

There are a range of other skills and knowledge needed, which we have touched on in different areas of this book, so we won't repeat ourselves.

6 | Career Possibilities

- The various specialisations available within the field of forensic psychology
- Range of possible employment settings/employers
- Possibilities within research and teaching
- Career possibilities in other countries

At this stage, it might be too early to suggest you should be fully aware of the range of opportunities available to you as a forensic psychologist! But what we can say is that if you're entering into this area, you should be thinking about how to gain practical experience or chances to 'shadow' those already working in the forensic field in order to enable you to make informed choices for the future and to secure a higher probability of gaining a trainee role.

Much later, you can then apply your specialist knowledge of psychological theory and the problems linked to criminal behaviour in order to work in a range of areas:

- Help to assess and rehabilitate offenders who are either in prisons or on parole, or who are patients in high-security hospitals
- Support and train prison staff and other professionals working within the criminal justice system
- Carry out research to improve and develop professional practice in the forensic field
- Support police investigations
- Teach and/or supervise others

DOI: 10.4324/9781315675831-6

You would work with offenders to help them understand and overcome their problems and to move towards changing some of their behaviour patterns. Your main duties might include:

- Carrying out specialist risk assessments for offenders
- Producing formal written reports for the courts
- Advising on the best location for prisoners
- Developing, delivering or evaluating treatment programmes for offenders with a view to reducing reoffending
- Offering expert advice to Parole Boards, mental health review tribunals or court cases
- Helping to write policies and strategies
- Training and mentoring new and trainee psychologists

You would work closely with a wide range of people, including prison officers, psychiatrists, offenders, children and high-risk offenders with severe personality disorders, or you may specialise in working with specific offender groups. You would also look for ways to reduce stress and improve life inside prisons for both staff and prisoners. You might do this by giving specialist advice on managing offenders or through workshops, for example, on issues such as coping with bullying. You might use a range of therapeutic techniques such as cognitive-behavioural therapy (CBT) or schema therapy to challenge the way some offenders view themselves and the world, and help them to make positive changes. You could be based in one setting or work across a number of sites, such as secure hospitals, prisons, rehabilitation units, secure and open residential units and police stations. You may also be required to visit courts and tribunals in order to provide expert witness testimony and would have had prior training to assist with this.

Training and Development

Many employers will actively encourage you to gain wider experience and develop skills in areas such as teaching, training and supervision. You will also receive regular clinical and professional mentoring from experienced colleagues.

You may choose to specialise, for example, in the assessment and treatment of sex offenders. You could undertake a research project leading to a PhD qualification, which would be helpful if you wanted to go into teaching or research as a career. You will need to ensure your CPD is kept up to date. You may move into more strategic and managerial roles and develop those skills.

Opportunities

The main employer of forensic psychologists is HMPPS. You could also work within the NHS (secure hospitals and rehabilitation units), Social Services Departments (including the Probation Service, the police and other secure settings) and in education (researching and teaching in higher education institutions).

You could go on to deliver and oversee psychology services in custody, pursue a policy- and strategy-based role or a management post focusing on a specific issue, such as developing strategies to reduce reoffending, or to increase safety for offenders and staff.

There are also opportunities for freelance and consultancy work, for example, as an expert witness, whilst in view of increasing student interest in forensic psychology, you could apply to become a university lecturer. This would enable you to teach students from an informed perspective whilst also encouraging and undertaking your own research, sometimes jointly with your students. Anyone new to teaching would be expected to enrol on an in-house part-time teaching and learning course to help develop their teaching skills.

To satisfy the requirements of continuing registration with the HCPC, you will need to take part in continuing professional development (CPD) activities that will keep your knowledge and skills up to date. This will also benefit your professional practice, which will be valuable for service users. The HCPC audits CPD activity every two years. Check the BPS website for details of their CPD approval scheme and online CPD planning and recording system, as this will save time in the long run.

You may find the following useful for vacancies and further reading:

- BPS Psychologist appointments
- NHS Jobs

- The Guardian (Jobs)
- HM Prison Service (vacancies)
- LGjobs
- Jobs Go Public
- Web sites (currently such as Indeed)

The HM Prison Service website provides video profiles of forensic psychologists and for more information on careers and vacancies.

Final Words

If you've made it this far and still think forensic psychology may be the career for you, then we hope this book has given you a flavour of how to get in, train and move forward with a career.

There are very many books written about forensic psychology in different settings. Whilst we've mentioned some theories and references, we have quite deliberately not tried to turn this into a book about forensic psychology itself. We hope we have hit the right balance, given that most of the queries we deal with are about the 'how do I. . . .' question.

If this is the right fit for you, it's a fabulous profession. If it's not, realising it sooner is helpful. But even if you realise it when you've invested time and effort, there are many different ways to use this profession. Never be afraid to change direction if something isn't for you – we spend far too much time at work for it to be the wrong fit – you may not find it straight away, but don't settle.

Always be learning – every day is a school day. We all make mistakes when we're training but also once qualified. This can be threatening for some to admit – but it's always better to admit it, put it right in whatever way possible and learn. Integrity as a psychological professional is key; don't walk past the unacceptable or compromise your values. Sometimes, aspects of the criminal justice system can impinge on what we believe is right – keep attuned to this and never cross whatever your red line is.

To talk about finding your 'why' and what gives you a purpose can sometimes sound a little grandiose. Psychology as a profession gives you a chance to make a difference – forensic psychology does that in many different ways in many different settings. We do hope you find the one that suits you.

Useful Information

Podcasts/YouTube:
The Forensic Psychology Podcast
www.audible.co.uk/podcast/The-Forensic-Psychology-Podcast/
  B08K5WGGSB

Let's Talk Forensic Psychology
www.youtube.com/c/LetsTalkForensicPsychology

Helpful websites:
HMPPS covers vacancies across the Prison and Probation
  Service and remains the single largest employer of forensic
  psychologists. Their website is now held under the Ministry
  of Justice (MoJ) website so the psychology posts can be tricky
  to find.

  - www.justice.gov.uk/jobs/prisons
  - https://prisonandprobationjobs.gov.uk/roles-at-hmpps/
    psychologist/

The National Careers Service (https://nationalcareers.service.
  gov.uk/job-profiles/forensic-psychologist) provides a very clear
  account of what a forensic psychologist does.

British Psychological Society is the professional body for
  psychologists.
British Psychological Society (BPS)
St Andrew's House

48 Princess Road East
Leicester
LE1 7DR
Tel: 0116 254 9568
www.bps.org.uk

The Health and Care Professions Council is the regulator for practitioner psychologists and other health professions and confers the title 'Forensic Psychologist' www.hcpc-uk.org/

References and Further Reading

Bandura, A. (1977). Self efficacy: Toward a unifying theory of behavioral change. *Psychology Review*, *84*(2), 191–215. https://doi.org/10.1037/0033-295X.84.2.191

Bandura, A., & National Inst of Mental Health. (1986). *Social foundations of thought and action: A social cognitive theory*. Prentice-Hall, Inc.

Bottoms, A. (1996). *Sexism and the female offender*. Gower Publishing.

Briere, J., & Runtz, M. (1988). Symptomatology associated with childhood sexual victimization in a nonclinical adult sample. *Child Abuse & Neglect*, *12*(1), 51–59. https://doi.org/10.1016/0145-2134(88)90007-5

British Psychological Society (2024). Standards for the accreditation of masters and doctoral programmes in forensic psychology masters & doctoral programmes in Forensic Psychology Accreditation Standards open for public consultation | BPS.

Broidy, L., & Agnew, R. (1997). Gender and crime: A general strain theory perspective. *The Journal of Research in Crime and Delinquency*, *34*(3), 275–306. https://doi.org/10.1177/0022427897034003001

Chesney-Lind, M. (1997). *The female offender: Girls, women, and crime*. Sage Publications.

Crewe, B. (2007). Power, adaptation and resistance in a late-modern men's prison. *British Journal of Criminology*, *47*(2), 256–275. https://doi.org/10.1093/bjc/azl044

Eisenberg, N., & Mussen, P. H. (1989). *The roots of prosocial behavior in children*. Cambridge University Press.

Finkelhor, D. (1984). *Child sexual abuse: New theory and research*. New York Free Press.

Gibbs, J. C., Basinger, K. S., & Fuller, D. (1992). *Moral maturity: Measuring the development of sociomoral reflection*. Lawrence Erlbaum Associates, Inc.

Hall, G. C. N., & Hirschman, R. (1992). Sexual aggression against children: A conceptual perspective of etiology. *Criminal Justice and Behavior*, *19*(1), 8–23. https://doi.org/10.1177/0093854892019001003

Hargie, O., & Tourish, D. (Eds.). (2000). *Handbook of communication audits for organisations*. Routledge.

Harrower, J. (2014). Becoming a qualified forensic psychologist. *Forensic update annual compendium.* British Psychological Society.

Hollin, C., & Howell, K. (1989). *Psychology and crime: An introduction to criminological psychology.* Routledge.

Kahneman, D., Slovic, P. and Tversky, A. (eds.) (1982). *Judgment under Uncertainty: Heuristics and Biases.* Cambridge: Cambridge University Press.

Kohlberg, L. (1976). Moral stages and moralization: The cognitive-development approach. In T. Lickona (Ed.), *Moral development and behavior: Theory and research and social issues* (pp. 31–53). Holt, Rienhart, and Winston.

Loeber, R., & Farrington, D. P. (2014). Age-crime curve. In G. Bruinsma & D. Weisburd (Eds.), *Encyclopedia of criminology and criminal justice* (pp. 12–18). Springer.

Loeber, R., Keenan, K., Lahey, B. B., Green, S. M., & Thomas, C. (1993). Evidence for developmentally based diagnoses of oppositional defiant disorder and conduct disorder. *Journal of Abnormal Child Psychology, 21*(4), 377–410. https://doi.org/10.1007/bf0126160

Mews, A., Di Bella, L., & Purver, M. (2017). *Impact evaluation of the prison based core sex offender treatment programme.* Ministry of Justice.

Middleton, D., Elliott, I. A., Mandeville-Norden, R., & Beech, A. R. (2006). An investigation into the applicability of the Ward and Siegert Pathways Model of child sexual abuse with Internet offenders. *Psychology, Crime & Law, 12*(6), 589–603. https://doi.org/10.1080/10683160600558352

Middleton, D., Mandeville-Norden, R., & Hayes, E. (2009). Does treatment work with Internet sex offenders? Emerging findings from the internet sex offender treatment programme (i-SOTP). *Journal of Sexual Aggression, 15*(1), 5–19. https://doi.org/10.1080/13552600802673444

Moffitt, T. E. (1993). Adolescence-limited and life-course-persistent antisocial behavior: A developmental taxonomy. *Psychological Review, 100*(4), 674–701. https://doi.org/10.1037/0033-295X.100.4.674

Novaco, R. W. (1994). Anger as a risk factor for violence among the mentally disordered. In J. Monahan & H. J. Steadman (Eds.), *Violence and mental disorder: Developments in risk assessment* (pp. 21–59). The University of Chicago Press.

Rollnick, S., & Miller, W. R. (1995). What is motivational interviewing? *Behavioural and Cognitive Psychotherapy, 23*, 325–334.

Ross, R. R., & Fabiano, E. A. (1985). *Time to think: A cognitive model of delinquency prevention and offender rehabilitation.* Institute of Social Sciences and Arts.

Ward, T., & Siegert, R. J. (2002). Toward a comprehensive theory of child sexual abuse: A theory knitting perspective. December 2002. *Psychology, Crime & Law, 8*(4), 319–351. https://doi.org/10.1080/10683160208401823

Notes

2. What Does a Forensic Psychologist Do?

1 See www.BPS.org.uk/public/whats-is-psychology
2 www.bps.org.uk/member-microsites/division-forensic-psychology
3 For a fuller description of Parole Board processes, you might want to read some of the publications on the Parole Board website: www.gov.uk/government/organisations/parole-board or summaries by The Howard League www.prisonreformtrust.org.uk/forprisonersfamilies/prisoninformationpages
4 www.bps.org.uk/power-threat-meaning-framework
5 See the saferlivingfoundation.org
6 If you are interested in the area of psychometrics, then the BPS work on Test Standards might interest you – www.psychtesting.org.uk
7 For an overview of the 'risk need', see authors such as Andrews and Bonta – for example Andrews, D. A., Bonta, J., & Wormith, S. J. (2006). The recent past and near future of risk/need assessment. *Crime & Delinquency, 52*, 7–27.
8 The Child Exploitation and Online Protection Centre is an interesting source of information in this area.
9 The Good Lives Model is a strengths-based approach worth reading about – https://goodlivesmodel.com/information.shtml
10 Pat Carlen's work is useful here for those interested.
11 Effective interventions for Women offenders: A Rapid Evidence Assessment: https://assets.publishing.service.gov.uk/government/uploads/system/uploads/attachment_data/file/448859/effective-interventions-for-women-offenders.pdf
12 [ARCHIVED CONTENT] Home Office | The Corston Report: a review of women with particular vulnerabilities in the criminal justice system: https://webarchive.nationalarchives.gov.uk/ukgwa/20080107214032/www.homeoffice.gov.uk/documents/corston-report/

i See Chapter 4 for a full description of these, in terms of the BPS Qualification itself as a route to training to be a forensic psychologist.

ii Prisons have a number of security categories, and psychologists are sometimes asked to contribute to panels considering whether an individual is presenting as a sufficiently low risk to be reduced in the security category or indeed presenting as a sufficiently high risk to require an increase in security level.

iii The use of the term 'offender' generally receives a range of thoughts from commentators. It is a difficult label to shift. We tend to prefer to use the descriptive term that is relevant, so an individual incarcerated in prison is a prisoner whilst he/she is held there.

iv Therapeutic Communities (TCs) are structured, psychologically informed environments – they are places where the social relationships, structure of the day and different activities together are all deliberately designed to help people's health and well-being.

v PIPEs are 'psychologically informed and planned environments' – units developed for a particular purpose in which events, interactions and relationships are subject to discussion and scrutiny with an emphasis on considering psychological theories in the planning of the general day-to-day running of the unit.

vi Psychologists employed by health trusts may also work in custody in units such as PIPEs, which are co-funded between HMPPS and health, alongside HMPPS employed staff.

vii Juvenile offenders are more readily called 'young people' in the CJS but the term 'juvenile' tends to linger. Young People are aged in England and Wales from 10 to 17, given the age of criminal responsibility being 10. In Scotland, this is 12, and in Northern Ireland, is 10 also. This group is, of course, children. The use of the word children is increasing in organisational terms.

viii These may be psychological interventions or include a range of wider considerations.

ix And, is the term 'date-rapist' an acceptable one? Is that a moral, legal, ethical or professional response? What impact did reading that sentence have on your thoughts and feelings?

x Single domain of forensic remember – not those who are registered in forensic and additional domains.

3. Psychology Graduates – The Next Steps

i Some undergraduates try to link with forensic settings to carry out their dissertation. Be aware that these opportunities tend to be few and far between, especially given the competition with postgraduate students who are also wanting the same access.

4. Becoming a Trainee

i   At the time of writing, you do not have to be in a traditional 'trainee' post, although it may take a little longer if you aren't. But this may change; make sure you check the BPS qualification requirements on the website.

5. Starting Out – Entering the Work Environment

13 Professionalism in healthcare professionals – HCPC research report: www. hcpc-uk.org/globalassets/resources/reports/professionalism-in-health-care-professionals.pdf

14 See also the views of service users of psychologists in prisons in Inside Time and prisonerben.blogspot.com as well as Shingler, J. (2020). Psychologists as "the quiet ones with the power": Understanding indeterminate sentenced prisoners' experiences of psychological risk assessment in the United Kingdom. *Psychology, Crime and Law*, *26*(3), 1–22.

15 See the work around psychologists in prisons completed by Dr Jason Warr.

16 Rollnick, S., & Miller, W. R. (1995). What is motivational interviewing? *Behavioural and Cognitive Psychotherapy*, *23*, 325–334. provides a good starting point.

Index

Note: Numbers followed by letter (12x, 12y, 12z) indicate an endnote. Numbers in *italics* indicate a figure. Numbers in **bold** indicate a table. Numbers that are <u>underlined</u> indicate a box.

14–16; as distinct from forensic psychiatry 14; as distinct from forensic science 14; Health and Care Professions Council (HCPC) regulation of 16; interest in 11–16; strengths of 15–16; television shows about 12; work of 16; workforce 44–46; *see also* trainees
forensic science 14

gangs 39–40
GBC *see* 'Graduate Basis for Chartered Membership' of the BPS
GBR *see* 'Graduate Basis for Registration'
Gibbs, J. 34
'Graduate Basis for Chartered Membership' of the BPS (GBC) 3–4, 8, 51, 52, 54
'Graduate Basis for Registration' (GBR) 4
Graduate Psychology Careers 3–6

Hall, N. 36
Hargie, O. 118
Harrower, J.: article in *Forensic Update Annual Compendium* 2014 91, 97
HCPC *see* Health and Care Professions Council
Health and Care Professions Council (HCPC) 16–17, 44; approved courses and programmes 52–53, *54*; BPS different from 57–61; HCPC data relating to forensic psychologists **44**, 45; HCPC-registered psychologists, forensic psychologists, and prison population by ethnicity 46, **46**; registering with 52
high-intensity OBPs 23
high-risk: cases 24; offenders 121
high-security hospitals 120

Hirschman, R. 36
His Majesty's Prison and Probation Service (HMPPS) 22–25
HMPPS *see* His Majesty's Prison and Probation Service
Hollin, C. 42
Howell, K. 42

internet sex offenders 36
Internet Sexual Offences Treatment Programme (i-SOTP) 37
I-SOTP *see* Internet Sexual Offences Treatment Programme (i-SOTP)

juvenile offenders 32–36, 129vii

Kahneman, D. 118
Kohlberg, L. 34

Listener Scheme 62
Loeber, R. 34

'mad' not 'bad', women offenders as 38
MI *see* motivational interviewing
Miller, William 188
Moffitt, T. 34
moral development in children: three levels of 34
moral development theory 34
moral reasoning: delinquency and 34
motivational interviewing (MI) 118
multiple clients 43
Mussen, P. 34

Novaco, R. 42

OBPs *see* offending behaviour programmes
offenders 11, 13; adolescent-limited 34; 'Circle of Support and Accountability' around 62; extremist 40–42; interviewing 117–119; life-course persistent

99–112; BPS route for 90–98;
career possibilities for 120–123;
comments of trainees and
registered forensic psychologists
regarding obtaining a post
69–70; competition for role of
50–51; core roles (1–4) of 91–98;
eligibility requirements for 68;
employed as 64; employment
application process as 71–72;
entering the work environment
113–119; independent route
followed by 64–66; interviewing
for a job by (what potential
employers are looking for) 72–81;
life as 81–89; non-trainee posts for
68; pathways for 63; placement
for 5–6, 53, 63, 65–66, 68, 71,
88–89, 98; placement handbook
for 99; Standards of Proficiency
99; starting out as 113–119;
training of 89; university routes
for 98–112; useful information for
124–125; wishes to help future
trainees 84, 84; working as 63,
67–71

UCAS *see* University College
    Admission Service
University College Admissions
    Service (UCAS): website 6, 7, 8

victim and perpetrator: dynamic
    between 37; working with 69, 87
victimisation 13, 31
victimology 49
victims: consequences of crimes on
    56; direct 13; potential 30; women
    as victims of domestic violence 38

Ward, T. 36; *see also* Pathways Model
Witmer, Lightner 2, 10
women as criminal offenders 38–39
women as victims of domestic
    violence 38
work experience 61–62

YJB *see* Youth Justice Board
YOT *see* Youth Offending Teams
young offenders 32–36
Youth Justice Board (YJB) 26, 33, 75
Youth Offending Service 69
Youth Offending Teams (YOT) 26, 35

For Product Safety Concerns and Information please contact our EU
representative GPSR@taylorandfrancis.com
Taylor & Francis Verlag GmbH, Kaufingerstraße 24, 80331 München, Germany